VGM Careers for You Series

CAREERS FOR

NATURE LOVERS
& Other
Outdoor Types

Louise Miller

Second Edition

VGM Career Books

Chicago   New York   San Francisco   Lisbon   London   Madrid   Mexico City
Milan   New Delhi   San Juan   Seoul   Singapore   Sydney   Toronto

Library of Congress Cataloging-in-Publication Data

Miller, Louise, 1940–
      Careers for nature lovers & other outdoor types / Louise Miller—2nd ed.
          p.   cm. — (VGM careers for you series)
      ISBN 0-658-01069-7 — ISBN 0-658-01070-0 (pbk.)
        1. Conservation of natural resources—Vocational guidance.
2. Environmental protection—Vocational guidance.   3. Biology—Vocational
guidance.   I. Title: Careers for nature lovers and other outdoor types.
II. Title.   III. Series.

S945.M55   2001
333.7′2′023—dc21   2001017891

VGM Career Books

*A Division of The **McGraw·Hill** Companies*

  2 3 4 5 6 7 8 9 0 LBM/LBM 0 9 8 7 6 5 4 3 2

ISBN 0-658-01069-7 (hardcover)
     0-658-01070-0 (paperback)

This book was set in Goudy Old Style by ImPrint Services
Printed and bound by Lake Book

McGraw-Hill books are available at special quantity discounts to use as premiums
and sales promotions, or for use in corporate training programs. For more
information, please write to the Director of Special Sales, Professional Publishing,
McGraw-Hill, Two Penn Plaza, New York, NY 10121-2298. Or contact your local
bookstore.

This book is printed on acid-free paper.

To the privilege of sharing life
with two members of another
(thankfully not endangered)
species—Baby and Buster, my
daily connection with nature
at its loving best.

Contents

Foreword   vii

CHAPTER ONE
Can This Planet Be Saved?   1

CHAPTER TWO
Careers in the Biological Sciences   13

CHAPTER THREE
Down on the Farm   39

CHAPTER FOUR
Planning the Land for Use   57

CHAPTER FIVE
Taking Care of the Forests and
Other Natural Resources   75

CHAPTER SIX
Careers in the Geosciences   95

CHAPTER SEVEN
The Need for Pollution Control and
Waste Management   111

About the Author   135

Foreword

With environmental issues such as global warming, ozone depletion, and tropical deforestation increasingly in the news, it should come as no surprise that Americans are more concerned about the environment than ever before. For the first time, Americans are realizing that our quality of life depends largely on the quality of the environment. And more and more people want to do something about it.

This interest in environmental issues may be recent, but our appreciation for nature is nothing new. We have always valued the scenic beauty of our national parks, forests, and natural areas. We treasure the diversity of plants and animals that inhabit these unspoiled places. And we find a special tranquility and connection with nature in these settings.

If you share this love of nature—and share the desire to preserve the natural world—you may wish to transform your interest into a career. *Careers for Nature Lovers* can help by offering information on a wide array of jobs in fields as diverse as biology, agriculture, land management, forestry, geology, and waste management. What's more, these aren't office jobs; as you will discover, this book focuses on employment opportunities that actually involve working outdoors.

You'll find details about jobs for geoscientists who study natural disasters such as earthquakes and for pollution control technicians who monitor industry's compliance with government pollution regulations. You'll find out about jobs for zoologists who work to save endangered species and for foresters who manage our national parks. Not only do these professions get you outside, working on the ground, but they can also make a crucial difference in stemming the environmental degradation that threatens our magnificent natural heritage.

I often tell people that being president of The Nature Conservancy is the best job in the world, in large part because I get to travel frequently to the Conservancy's system of thirteen hundred nature preserves in the United States and its cooperative projects beyond our borders. But when I'm visiting these beautiful places, I usually find myself envious of the preserve managers and land stewards. These are the people who are really on the cutting edge of environmental protection. Men and women working in the outdoors for the outdoors are the ones who are getting things done and making a difference for us and for generations to come.

> John C. Sawhill
> Former President
> The Nature Conservancy

In Memoriam

John Sawhill passed away as this second edition was being prepared. He was a leader with vision and commitment who had the courage to write the foreword to this book even before the first edition was published. Gregory Low, vice president for U.S. conservation for the Nature Conservancy, and the author thought it would be a fitting tribute to John's memory to include his original words in this revised edition.

CHAPTER ONE

Can This Planet Be Saved?

Our incredible Earth, natural habitat and nurturing ground for so many species, has its limits, as do all the species that call it home. The protection of the planet's water, land, and air has become increasingly important to the ecological balance of all life on Earth.

We are bombarded on a daily basis with news of perils to our habitat: scientists theorize about global warming, parents worry about their children's health, whole species are threatened to the point of extinction, food supplies are contaminated, oil continues to spill into our water sources, rain forests are depleted at a rapid rate, animals are displaced from their natural environments because of land development.

In addition, waste materials are thrown into landfills, nuclear waste may be stored in public areas, and public lands are often privatized for development or logging. Some scientists now believe that Mars once had life and the elements that sustain it—water and an atmosphere—which supports the theory that planets can literally die. Maybe even Earth.

Why Does Biodiversity Matter?

Biodiversity comes from the two-word phrase *biological diversity*, which refers to the variety of species of plants and animals and the ways they interrelate in ecosystems and interact with the environment. The loss of habitat, decline or overexploitation of a species, introduction of a foreign substance, pollution and contamination, and global climate changes upset the delicate balance of nature. All life is interdependent, and human beings—our food supply, the air we breathe, the water we drink—are affected, too, when biodiversity and ecosystems are threatened. Ecologists are those who research conservation and restoration of ecosystems, including the effects of land uses and management practices, in order to understand which processes affect the loss of various species.

What Each of Us Can Do

On a personal level, you may think that you cannot do much to understand, let alone reverse, any harm that has already been done to our environment or prevent further damage from occurring. It all seems like an overwhelming job; even so, you have taken some steps on a daily basis to "reduce, reuse, and recycle." You shop for goods with no extraneous packaging that would be thrown away. You recycle paper, plastic, glass, and cans. You wrap your presents in recycled paper products and take public transportation, carpool, or bike to work or school. You eat organic foods when possible and actively participate in the annual Earth Day celebrations. You probably even belong to Greenpeace, the Sierra Club, or other environmental organizations. You have determined that our precious Earth can be saved if everyone takes these small steps.

We are aware that some of the natural resources available to us today may not be there for our children or grandchildren to enjoy. But we also know that we hold in our hands the power to stop—even to reverse—the damage that has been done to the environment if we all act in concert in everyday ways for the rest of our lives.

Working to Save the Earth

You are ready to take the next step—making a living working for and with the natural environment. You want to contribute even more to the preservation of the natural resources that once were so abundant but that now are threatened. If you would literally like to "save the Earth," you may be interested in exploring the many jobs available to you.

Some of the jobs we will discuss require advanced education and training; others may not. Careers may deal primarily with the land, water, air, plants, or animals. Some may overlap. Some jobs will take you to the city, the ocean, farmland, mountains, or parks. Many jobs will require a high degree of scientific knowledge and expertise. In those cases, your education will play a major role in your decision.

Federal, state, county, and municipal government agencies offer a wide range of opportunities in the environmental field. Private industry, independent organizations, and corporations also have departments that are devoted to studying and analyzing compliance with environmental regulations. The various requirements, criteria, educational standards, and degrees of commitment within these organizations should help you decide where you want to work.

The Global View

We know that a natural disaster, such as an oil spill or a nuclear accident, may have global consequences. A worldwide approach is essential to the preservation of our natural resources. Thanks to advances in technology, instant communication around the world is possible. The Internet has connected the human population as never before, and we are all part of the World Wide Web of information, knowledge, facts, and discussion. This global awareness and access creates new opportunities for working for the environment.

Using the Internet

For anyone willing to explore cyberspace, the Internet offers an array of useful information on career opportunities around the world working with the environment. By typing a few keywords pertinent to your area of interest into a search engine, a world of information will open up to you. If you do not have a computer at home, you can use one in your local library or school. Your local library is also a depository of books, magazines, newspapers, and possibly videos and CD-ROMs that contain information on environmental careers.

Is Environmental Work for You?

You are probably already on the right track for choosing a career in the environment if you currently take everyday steps to restore the ecological balance and if you have checked out the Internet or local library for more career information. Now you may be ready to start asking yourself some basic questions to help determine the environmental career that's right for you.

1. Could you work outdoors, no matter what the weather?

2. Which area would you like to work with: land, water, air, plants, or animals?

3. How much time and money are you willing to invest in your education?

4. Do you work well as part of a team?

5. Do you communicate well both orally and in writing?

6. Are you interested in the sciences as a field of study?

7. Would you prefer to work for the government, a private conservation organization, or a corporation?

8. Are you willing to relocate to another state, province, or country?

Since the environment provides you with a variety of career opportunities, you will have to make decisions based on your answers to these questions. Many jobs are done outdoors, sometimes in the worst kind of weather. Some jobs require physical strength and fitness. Others require a great deal of education and training, and your inclination toward certain subjects may determine which career you will choose.

Where Do You Start?

If you are in school now, you should start thinking seriously about courses you should take and adjust your curriculum accordingly. Talk to career counselors, check the Internet, write to governmental agencies and private environmental organizations, read about your career choice, and perform volunteer work in your chosen field. The more education and experience you have, the better your chances for employment. For some jobs, a master's degree may be required, as well as on-the-job training. You should investigate colleges and universities that are known for excellence in the courses you need to complete your degree.

If you have ever played a team sport, you know whether you are a good team player. If you are still in school, you may be a member of a debating team, glee club, or the yearbook staff. These are all groups of people who have to work together for a common goal. If you work in an office or have volunteered for a community organization, you have also been a team member.

Scientists and experts often have to work together across disciplines to solve an environmental problem, so if you work well with others and are willing to share your results, you have the qualities needed for a team player.

Excellent communication skills and computer literacy are vitally important in any job that involves sharing information. You may be called upon to write reports, results, and recommendations of your field investigations for your supervisor or even for the public.

Since environmental jobs often require strenuous outdoor work under less than desirable conditions, you will have to be more physically fit than you would for a sedentary office job. You should review your health and fitness routines to be sure that you could endure the more physical work that may be demanded of you.

Some of the jobs that you may apply for could be located far from home. Many environmental jobs are found in national or state parks and forests. They may be located near a lake or ocean, on a farm, or in the mountains. The possibility of having to relocate in order to do the work you choose is something to think about as you explore the possibilities.

If you are changing careers, you will also have to assess your strengths and interests. You will have to determine the specific field you want to be in and the extent of education and training you will need. It may take a few years of night school to acquire the certificate, license, or degree that you need, but the time and effort will be well worth it when you're finally doing work you love—and helping to save the Earth as well.

Environmental Opportunities

To help you make your career decision, let's take a look at some of the opportunities available to you in this most important of career tracks—the preservation of Mother Earth and all her creatures!

Careers in Biology

If we define biology as the study of living things, we can see how all-encompassing careers in the biological sciences can be. They include everything from aquatic biologists to soil scientists, from botanists to toxicologists, from game managers to horticulturists. Biologists are employed in forests, agricultural research stations, ocean ships, and farms. If you choose biology for a career, you will need at least a high school diploma or bachelor's degree. With a master's or doctoral degree, a solid, long-term career is almost assured. So start studying now to be a botanist, physiologist, biochemist, zoologist, ecologist, or horticulturist, and you will enter the wonderful world of the biological scientist. Your chances for a rewarding career are excellent.

Landscape Architecture

Landscape architects are on-site specialists in the analysis of land features, vegetation, and geography for use in the design of projects in forests, parks, and subdivisions and for airports and highways. Landscape architects are employed by local governments, corporations, or engineering firms. Others are self-employed, often as consultants.

Land developers work closely with landscape architects to assure that the land is suitable for the particular project that they are planning and that environmental regulations are complied with. In addition to a bachelor's degree, you may also need a state license if you want to practice independently.

Forestry Work

You may also want to consider the possibility of becoming a forest ranger or manager. Much of the United States is forest land,

and a chief obligation of a forester is to prevent fires and to be generally responsible for the proper maintenance of the trees in a forest and the safety of visitors. The forest manager assumes larger responsibilities according to the uses of the forest; that is, whether the forest is used as a wildlife refuge or for the production of lumber.

Conservation scientists—such as fish culturists, wildlife biologists, technicians, wardens, and animal rehabilitators, as well as ornithologists, ecologists, and wildlife managers—are also employed in parks and forests throughout the country. Since the forest houses so many different life forms and can be used for different purposes, you may find your niche here.

Geological Sciences

Geology and related geosciences may intrigue you as a possible career track. The government, private industry, architectural firms, and oil companies all employ geologists. More and more, geologists are becoming involved in environmental work, including pollution and waste management. A solid background in mathematics and science is necessary whether you decide to work as an engineering geologist, marine geologist, hydrologist, or mineralogist. A bachelor's degree is the minimum requirement, and a master's degree is needed for some positions.

Waste Management and Pollution Control

Areas of environmental work that are becoming increasingly important are waste management and pollution control. Many efforts have been made over the past several years to try to alleviate the problems of open dumping of garbage into landfills. These dumps can eventually contaminate groundwater and provide a base for spreading disease.

There will always be garbage, but local governments and private organizations are employing engineers, chemists, toxicologists, inspectors, and analysts to come up with safe ideas for waste management and to try to recover energy and natural resources. Both government and private industry must also comply with a body of regulations that have been enacted to protect the environment. One way of dealing with waste is, of course, through recycling of plastic, glass, paper, and aluminum. A whole new avenue of careers has grown out of this aspect of waste management, and it also offers new career opportunities.

Where the Jobs Are

As we know, employment for the various careers working with the environment is available through federal, state, and local governments; private industry; and independent, grassroots organizations. Federal employing agencies involved in some aspect of the environment are the Environmental Protection Agency, U.S. Fish and Wildlife Service, U.S. Forest Service, U.S. Bureau of Mines, Bureau of Land Reclamation, National Park Service, U.S. Geological Survey, the Nuclear Regulatory Commission, and the Smithsonian Environmental Research Center. Individual states employ environmental workers in their departments of natural resources, environmental protection, fish and wildlife, ecology, or pollution control. County and municipal agencies often have similar offices.

Independent and grassroots organizations, such as Greenpeace, Center for Neighborhood Technology, Wilderness Society, Save-the-Redwoods League, Friends of the Earth, and the National Association of Environmental Professionals may also serve as valuable career sources in your pursuit of an environmental career. Private corporations advertise in local and national newspapers, trade publications, and professional newsletters.

Your local library should have a copy of *Encyclopedia of Associations*, which lists professional organizations within the various disciplines. They, in turn, may lead you to specific educational and training requirements as well as employment opportunities in your chosen field. The *Occupational Outlook Handbook* describes professions and projects future needs. College and university job placement services and counselors may put you in touch with recruiters from industries and agencies that are hiring.

So the keys for opening up doors to a new and important career are at your disposal. Let's walk into this vast hall of possibilities to see if we've come to the right place and what we're going to do when we get there.

For Further Information

Associations

Convention on Biological Diversity
Secretariat
World Trade Centre
393 St. Jacques Street, Office 300
Montreal, QC H2Y 1N9
Canada
www.biodiv.org

Ecological Society of America
1707 H Street NW
Washington, DC 20006
http://esa.sdsc.edu

Publications

Occupational Outlook Handbook. U.S. Department of Labor, Bureau of Labor Statistics, Annual.

The Complete Guide to Environmental Careers for the 21st Century. Island Press, 1999.

Fasulo, Michael, and Paul Walker. *Careers in the Environment*. VGM Career Books, 2000.

CHAPTER TWO

Careers in the Biological Sciences

T he field of biology is so wide-ranging that, if you choose a career in the biological sciences, you are assured of a variety of possibilities. These are not just confined to working with microscopes and formaldehyde, as you might think from your experience in high school classes. If, for example, you choose to become a botanist, you'll be studying plant life; a zoologist, animal life; an ecologist, environmental relationships. As a physiologist, you would study life processes of living organisms.

If you want to work outdoors as a biologist, you may become a wildlife biologist or marine biologist, ornithologist or ichthyologist, herpetologist or mammalogist. You would work in forests and parks, zoos, agricultural research stations, at fish hatcheries, on ocean ships, or under water. You could also work at rehabilitation facilities.

Biology Careers

Wildlife Biologists

As a wildlife biologist, you would probably work for the government—federal, state, or local. On the federal level, the primary employers are the U.S. Fish and Wildlife Service of the Department of the Interior and the National Park Service. The

U.S. Forest Service is also a possibility as well as the Bureau of Sport Fisheries and the National Marine Fishery Service. Every state has a special department for the conservation of natural resources or environmental quality. Large cities or counties with a parks department may, on a limited basis, offer jobs for the wildlife biologist. Independent wildlife preservation societies, sanctuaries, rehabilitation centers, and game preserves also employ wildlife biologists.

What do wildlife biologists do? They are hired primarily to study habitat, heritage, and the survival needs of birds, animals, and other living organisms. They study the effects of relationships between species and the effects of pollutants and pesticides on these species. Wildlife biologists also keep track of animals, studying their migration habits, locations, and distribution. They have to study animals' diets and where they find their food, investigate how pollution affects their lives, and generally try to save species from extinction. Wildlife refuge managers are primarily concerned with the protection and preservation of both indigenous and migratory fish and wildlife and for setting policy for fishing and hunting.

As a wildlife biologist, you will need a college degree in biological sciences, including courses in mammalogy, ornithology, animal ecology, and wildlife management. you will also need to complete courses in comparative anatomy, physiology, general zoology, ecology, wildlife biology, and entomology.

Research Biologists

Whenever there is a variation in the natural environment, caused by such things as land development, temperature alterations, or swamp drainage, natural habitats will change. This has an impact on animal and plant life. Research biologists are concerned with fish and wildlife population, plant and animal interactions, and animal habitat requirements, especially regarding nutritional needs. Environmental impact statements often have to be prepared to determine whether certain development pro-grams should be attempted if animal and plant life will be destroyed or disrupted.

Fish Biologists

As part of wildlife management, you may choose to become a fish biologist. You would find jobs in a natural setting, such as a park or forest or hatchery. A large part of your work might be to preserve fish habitats by testing water for pollutants. You might spend time on a boat, calculating water volume and collecting fish samples and other organic materials. Based on this study, you could then estimate the fish supply for any given lake and plan accordingly.

To become a fishery biologist, you need to have a college degree in biological science with courses in limnology, fishery biology, aquatic botany, aquatic fauna, oceanography, fish cul-ture, or related courses. Other required courses include general zoology, vertebrate biology, comparative anatomy, physiology, or related subjects.

Marine and Aquatic Biologists

As a biologist, you may decide to work exclusively with organ-isms found in water rather than those found on land. You would be called a marine or aquatic biologist, and you might study plankton, mussels, and snails, among other organisms. Although some of your work would be done in the laboratory, you would have to collect actual samples from the water in order to study salt content, acidity, and oxygen level. You would be working with organisms in rivers, lakes, and oceans and would often have to dive into the water in order to gather needed materials to be analyzed.

Because of these on-site investigations, aquatic biologists are often called on to advise and make recommendations on environmental matters to other environmental specialists. These may include engineers, pest control specialists, and water pollution analysts or inspectors. Marine biologists may also work in conjunction with marine chemists, whose primary task is to study the organic composition of the ocean. They study changing chemical reactions affecting the food chain as well as the amount of carbon dioxide that is in the ocean. Marine biologists also investigate human waste to see how it affects sea life. As a marine biologist, you may also work with geologists, engineers, and oceanographers as well as a variety of technicians.

Marine Mammalogists

If you would like to work with marine mammals, you may be in for a difficult but rewarding career. Long days at sea, in laboratories, and at the computer, as well as feeding the animals and cleaning up after them, are part of the job. You could be a field biologist, fishery vessel observer, animal care specialist, trainer, whale watch guide naturalist, or conservation worker.

If you are interested in the field, you have a choice of educational paths: anatomy, physiology, ecology, molecular biology, genetics, veterinary medicine, or management. You will have to decide which marine mammals you would like to study, and whether you would like to work for government, industry, oceanaria, or private organizations. If you decide to study a specific species that is only found in a particular place, you may have to relocate to that place.

In high school, you should take biology, chemistry, physics, math, computer science, and English. You will need a B.S. in biology, chemistry, physics, geology, or psychology for an entry-level position. A minor in science, computer science, math, statistics, or engineering could help you in pursuing your career. Be sure to continue to develop your oral and written communications skills. Since you may be interested in mammals in other parts of the world, a second language would also be helpful. The bachelor's degree will allow you to become a field technician, consultant for industry, or animal care specialist.

You should also consider going on to graduate school if you want to specialize in marine mammal science. Here you can be a little creative. For example, it may be useful to think about a degree in statistics if you want to study population patterns. Or you could study environmental law or engineering, depending on your particular interest. Your master's degree could help you design research projects, supervise field studies, or head up training programs. Your doctorate would qualify you for coordinating government and corporate projects or management of oceanaria.

Whichever path you choose, it is a good idea to acquire some practical experience as a volunteer at a local or government organization. Zoos, museums, and oceanaria may have internships that will give you skills and will help you discover whether this is the field for you. Internships also help you establish a network of people who may recommend you for schools or jobs.

The *Chronicle of Higher Education* and *Science* list available positions, and the human resource departments of individual agencies and companies will post available jobs. Professional associations, scientific conferences, and electronic bulletin boards such as MARMAN, WHALENET, and OMNET also list job openings.

Oceanographers

The word *oceanographer* applies to ocean scientists, engineers, and technicians who investigate how the ocean works. A degree in oceanography will include the study of physics, chemistry, biology, and geology. Ocean studies tend to be interdisciplinary, though specialties exist.

Physical oceanographers specialize in ocean currents, how they are formed, and what energizes them. While they study light, radar, heat, sound, and wind, their main interests lie in the interaction between the ocean and atmosphere, sea, weather, and climate. Chemical oceanographers concern themselves with chemical compounds and their interactions and the impact on ocean chemistry of natural and man-made materials. Biological oceanographers explore the interrelationships of oceanic life forms and energy sources, including the human impact on these life forms.

Geological and geophysical oceanographers study the sediments and rocks on the sea floor. Their observations concern the movement of suspended sediment, the movement of materials on the sea floor, and biological and chemical interactions. Although most oceanographers are basic scientists, they can also be mathematicians or meteorologists. Ocean technicians—who calibrate equipment, take measurements and samples, and repair and maintain instruments—are also vital to oceanography.

Oceanography is a very specialized field and requires at least a bachelor's degree, and a career in ocean science requires a master's degree and, in some cases, a doctorate. If you are in college and are preparing to be an oceanographer, you have some serious study ahead of you. Physics, chemistry, biology, geology, geophysics, and even meteorology, math, and engineering are courses you should consider. Many universities offer individual courses in pertinent subjects, including graduate programs in oceanography.

Eos, the publication of the American Geophysical Union, advertises employment opportunities, as does *Sea Technology* and the Marine Technology Society's *Journal*. The federal government offers employment through the following agencies:

- U.S. Department of Energy

- Minerals Management Serivice

- U.S. Geological Survey of the Department of Interior

- National Oceanic and Atmospheric Administration of the Department of Commerce

- National Research Foundation

- Naval Oceanographic Office

- Naval Research Laboratory

- Office of Naval Research

Knowledge of the oceans is important for weather and climate information, defense and transportation purposes, and for the study of new food and drug sources. Oceanographers have the power to improve the use of water sources to promote healthy conditions for the species that depend on them. Good communications skills, common sense, and a passion for your work should land you a lasting career in oceanography.

Botanists

Botanists specialize in the biology of plants and can work in conservation, natural resources management, agriculture, forestry, horticulture, medicine, or biotechnology. As a botanist, you may further specialize. Plant physiologists study the chemistry and inner workings of plants. Plant ecologists study plants in their natural environments. Pathologists study plant diseases, and taxonomists study plant diversity and classification. Agronomists specialize in farm crops and grasses. You may work in laboratories or in the field, alone or with other scientists. Some areas you may be involved with include:

- the study of the environment on plants

- the revision of classifications of plants as a result of lab or field work

- the development of new drugs and medicine derived from plants

- the identification of new plants

- the use of computers to analyze data and develop databases

Biotechnologists

A comparatively new field is biotechnology, which includes the controversial technology of splicing genes from one species into a species that is not directly related. This transference of genes is intended to produce pest- and virus-resistant crops and improve the efficiency of meat and food production. These foods are referred to as GMOs, genetically modified organisms, or GEs, genetically engineered species, because they are not the result of natural evolution.

Some people are concerned because the impact of GMOs on human health in the long run is unknown. Their impact on the environment is also in question. Agricultural and pharmaceutical companies as well as government agencies employ biotechnologists and genetic engineers, but public outcry about GMOs and their possible hazards to human health and the environment in general could affect the job market.

Among the other career paths for biotechnologists are greenhouse assistant and plant breeder. To be a greenhouse assistant, you would need a high school diploma or an associate's degree. You would observe horticultural or pest problems and try to correct them. You would record and analyze data and interpret results of these tasks. A plant breeder needs a bachelor's degree or equivalent. As a breeder you would design, develop, and implement research projects, usually as part of a team.

Biotechnology represents a growing industry in the United States, and salaries and benefits in biotech companies are usually competitive.

Zoological Careers

Most of us have been to the zoo at one time or another. Maybe we went because the only animals we had ever seen were cats, dogs, an occasional cow or horse, maybe some robins or sparrows. But zebras, giraffes, elephants, or baboons? Hardly likely. The exotic animals, birds, and snakes from Asia, South America, and Africa were there to entertain and amuse us. It was a great place to go with the family on a summer Sunday. Besides, we could usually get some cotton candy, popcorn, and ice cream all in one day.

At one time, all zoo animals were in cages, usually only with members of their own species. Sometimes the architecture would not allow you to see the animals you came to view.

But the purpose and function of the zoo have changed in the last fifty years—often for environmental reasons. Many natural habitats have been destroyed because of land development and pollution, and whole species have become endangered, if not extinct. Modern zoos are trying to recreate natural environments and conserve species by duplicating as closely as possible flora and fauna of their habitats and breeding in captivity those animals that are endangered. They are then often released to special reserves or forests.

Typically, today's zoo will have a bird house, a monkey house, and a great ape house. Other areas will house hoofed animals, elephants, giraffes, lions, tigers, sea lions, beavers, bears, and otters. Amphibians, reptiles, birds, and invertebrates are also often included. Habitats such as wetlands, creeks, and small forests are also found in zoos. Most zoos also have educational and ecological exhibits and research and breeding facilities.

Since more and more zoological parks are becoming "bioparks," much of the work is done outside with the animals. Biologists, botanists, ecologists, ornithologists, mammalogists, physiologists, and zoologists work together to try to create an environment that might come close to that which we have almost destroyed.

Zoologists

Those of you who wish to work for the conservation, protection, and preservation of individual animals and whole species may choose to become zoologists. Zoologists of today may also be working toward the so-called biological parks of the future where more plants, water animals, and other scientific innovations will further transform the zoological park.

The zoologist has the responsibility of planning the future of the collection, maintaining records, and obtaining necessary permits and licenses. Research zoologists are more involved with the ecology and behavior of the animals and seek ways to improve their care. Research may also involve reproduction and breeding in captivity.

Since zoologists study the structures, ecology, functions, and habitats of animals, their knowledge can be applied to wildlife management, conservation, medicine, and agriculture. As a zoologist, you may specialize in entomology (study of insects), ecology (study of environment), ichthyology (study of fish), ornithology (study of birds), herpetology (study of reptiles), mammalogy (study of mammals), or ethology (study of animal behavior).

You may be called on to design programs to increase the population of endangered wild or captive animals or to prepare wildlife awareness programs for the general public. As a zoologist, you will have to be observant, logical, and a team worker.

You don't have to be confined to working in a zoo if you decide to become a zoologist. Federal and state wildlife management and conservation agencies such as the U.S. Fish and Wildlife Service, the U.S. Forest Service, and the U.S. Bureau of Land Management have jobs for zoologists.

Zookeepers

Zookeepers work closely with the animals on a daily basis. They feed and water the animals in their care, keep the enclosures clean, and administer medicine under a veterinarian's supervision. They often have to transport animals, keep records on their behavior, and communicate with the public about a variety of species. The zookeeper may specialize in infants or mothers of the newborn or a specific species. You will need to earn a bachelor's degree in animal behavior, animal science, conservation biology, marine biology, wildlife, or zoology to become a zookeeper.

The American Association of Zoo Keepers sets standards for animal care workers in the United States and Canada. It holds conferences, and specific chapters sponsor activities that allow networking possibilities. The American Zoo and Aquarium Association provides lists of employers, and the American Association of Zoological Parks and Aquariums is another organization that might provide opportunities for sharing ideas with other animal caretakers.

Other Positions

If you choose to work in an outside job in a zoological park, you could work as a gardener, tree worker, or maintenance worker. These workers are also needed in parks, science centers, and aquariums.

Ecological Careers

Of all the career opportunities we have looked at so far, that of the ecologist is the one that brings together the study of all natural systems—earth, air, water, plants, and animals. Connections between living organisms and effects of their interactions are ecologists' concerns. Much of the ecologist's work is alone outside—on the ocean, in a rain forest, or in an urban setting. That means that they work in all climates throughout the year. They may then be called upon to work in the laboratory to analyze data and write reports and recommendations based on their study. The balance of nature, wherever it occurs, is what they investigate and analyze.

Aquatic Ecologists

Aquatic ecologists observe plant and animal life in or near natural bodies of water. Many factors affect marine life, including the water's temperature, toxicity, and acidity, as well as light and oxygen levels. Whether you work with saltwater or freshwater, your main concern will be the ecological balance of aquatic ecosystems—how plants and animals live in that particular environment.

Plant Ecologists

Plant ecologists apply many of the same principles to plant life and study those factors—such as temperature, rainfall, soil content, and elevation—that affect the plant's life cycles. The reproductive life of plants as well as their population patterns and economic worth are part of the plant ecologist's job. As a plant ecologist, you would be working with other professionals whose careers depend on an understanding of plants, such as agricultural scientists, foresters, rangers, and horticulturists.

Animal Ecologists

If you prefer to build your career around the interactions of animals with their environment, you will want to explore the field of animal ecology. These ecologists study not only the present status of animals and their environments but also their origin and history. The study of habitat and diseases as well as the particular geographical location is also a part of the work of the animal ecologist.

Animal ecologists also try to prevent animal extinction by studying, for example, the effects of pesticides on animal populations. Pesticides that are harmful to animals often have the same effects on humans, so studying their diseases may be very helpful to human and plant life.

Getting Started in Biology Careers

Now, how do you get started in this field? First, you probably have to be interested in science courses in high school. Advanced biology, chemistry, and physics courses are recommended as well as math, English, and computer science. While you are still in high school, it is a good idea to decide which career path appeals to you and choose a college that will fulfill the requirements of your choice. At this time, it may also be good to take a cold, hard look at employment possibilities to help you make the right decision.

Because of our highly technological society, the nature lover with the highest degree of education will probably get the best job. However, if you have just a high school diploma, you could get a job as a greenhouse aide, animal care assistant, landscape gardener, or tree worker. With two years of college or some technical training, you could become a technician or warden. Biologists, botanists, zoologists, biotechnologists, and ecologists, however, should have at least a bachelor's degree. For some careers, or for advancement in your career track, a master's degree or doctorate is essential.

It is important for you to know that, although you may do most of your work in the great outdoors, you may also be called on to write reports and recommendations, to work with others on team projects, and occasionally to communicate directly with the public. For example, you may testify at public hearings or make public decisions based on your knowledge or fieldwork. A well-rounded education will prepare you for all these eventualities and provide expanded opportunities for advancement.

Where to Find the Jobs

As we have seen, the federal government is a major employer of environmental workers, but you will also find jobs at the state, county, and municipal level of government. Corporations are also becoming more and more involved in environmental impact regulations and are therefore hiring biologists to help them comply with government regulations. Independent grassroots and nonprofit organizations hire biologists only on a limited basis but should be looked into for possible career opportunities.

Federal Jobs for Biological Scientists

The U.S. Department of the Interior (DOI) manages more than ninety-four million acres of land and water. It administers five hundred national wildlife refuges, sixty-five fish hatcheries, thirty-eight wetland districts, and fifty wildlife coordination areas. Its many programs encompass migratory birds, endangered species, wildlife refuge management, marine mammals, law enforcement, Great Lakes fisheries, foreign government coordination, and self-guided nature trails. Most careers for biologists will be found at the U.S. Fish and Wildlife Service (USFWS).

Habitat Conservation Division

The Division of Habitat Conservation of the USFWS supports programs that prevent the degradation of fish and wildlife habitats. This division is involved in providing habitat planning and technical assistance, working with other organizations to restore habitats on public and private lands, conserving threatened coastal habitats, and mapping and monitoring this country's wetlands.

Through its project planning program activities, the division tries to ensure that federal projects such as navigation and flood control minimize harmful impacts on fish and wildlife. These activities are also designed to protect declining species from becoming endangered. The division investigates permits and licenses for the Army Corps of Engineers and the Forest Service and reviews the environmental activities of all federal agencies to see that they do not adversely affect fish and wildlife.

The division also works on a habitat restoration program that provides technical and financial help to private landowners to help restore or improve fish or wildlife habitats on their property. This program is based on a minimum ten-year voluntary agreement with the property owner.

The division's coastal program works with state and local governments and private organizations to conserve habitats of fish and wildlife along this country's extensive coasts. Because of the dense populations on our coasts, restoration and management programs are necessary for fish and wildlife protection. The National Coastal Wetlands Conservation Grant Program, established in 1990, provides matching grants to coastal states for the acquisition, restoration, or enhancement of those lands. And the Branch of Habitat Assessment has formulated ecological databases of scientific and technical information to help resource managers make appropriate policy decisions regarding fish and wildlife habitats.

The USWFS also is responsible for the management of polar bears, walruses, sea and marine otters, manatees, and dugong. Part of its job is to enforce the Marine Mammal Protection Act's moratorium on taking and importing marine mammals and their parts.

Fisheries Program

The USFWS fisheries program has six stated priorities:

1. Recovering listed and candidate aquatic species

2. Restoring interjurisdictional fisheries and aquatic ecosystems

3. Managing interjurisdictional fisheries

4. Fulfilling mitigation obligations

5. Restoring depleted aquatic populations to preclude listing

6. Providing fish and wildlife management assistance to tribes and on USFWS lands

The USFWS National Fish Hatchery System, established in 1871, is responsible for the conservation, restoration, enhancement, and management of U.S. fishery resources and aquatic ecosystems. The system was originally founded to provide food fish to replenish declining fish populations. Now it has integrated the fish hatcheries and fisheries management to improve conservation efforts. The system consists of sixty-six hatcheries, eight fish technology centers, and nine fish health centers.

The American Fisheries Society (AFS)

This society, founded in 1870, is a professional organization that promotes scientific research and encourages comprehensive education for fisheries scientists as well as on-the-job training. It is the oldest and largest such organization for fisheries scientists. It offers scientific meetings and certification programs, publishes research journals, and has programs on international and public affairs and public information.

Application for certification is ongoing, and you don't have to be a member to be certified. But certification is valuable for your employment or promotion, your demonstration of expertise, your continuing professional activities, and for verification of your professionalism.

If you apply for membership, you have to submit transcripts with course numbers from all the schools you have attended. There are fees for membership and for the actual certificate. The AFS website is www.fisheries.org; or write to 5410 Grosvenor Lane, Suite 110, Bethesda, MD 20814.

Obtaining a Federal Job

The primary employer of biologists in the United States is the U.S. Fish and Wildlife Service (USFWS) of the Department of the Interior (DOI). In order to become employed by this agency, you will have to register with the U.S. Office of Personnel Management (OPM). This office can give you information on eligibility requirements and available positions. The OPM administers testing offices where application forms are available.

You can access the DOI website at www.doi.gov and the USFWS and its Division of Habitat Conservation website at www.fws.gov.

Jobs with the federal government can also be accessed at www.usajobs.opm.gov, which provides general information and will help you create and send resumes on-line. This site outlines the three steps necessary to apply for a job with the federal government:

1. Use any of the automated parts of the system, including vacancies, application form, and resume preparation.

2. Receive announcements of vacancies, testing and educational requirements, and salary.

3. Follow directions for submitting a resume or F-612 form that includes job and personal information, education, work experience, and other qualifications.

If you do not have a computer at home, you can access these websites at your local library.

The OPM also publishes *The Qualifications Standards Handbook for General Schedule Positions*, which is also available at your library. The handbook spells out policies, educational and occupational requirements, knowledge and skills required, career tracks, and specialized experience. All federal employees are hired at a specific General Schedule, or GS, level.

The federal government grants preferences to veterans, some-times waiving requirements. These are also explained in the handbook. You will also find that the USFWS accepts applications that don't meet the requirements if you are within nine months of completing your requirements and can prove that you have completed the course work by the time you are hired. Higher education and more experience will generally qualify you for a higher GS level, which also means a higher salary.

Written tests are administered to most applicants and must be passed in order to register for a job. You should note that when many candidates apply for the same job, the agency suspends the registration process so that no new applicants can apply.

The Canadian Wildlife Service

Similar to the U.S. Department of the Interior, the Canadian Wildlife Service (CWS) is part of Environment Canada and was founded in the early 1900s primarily to protect the diminishing migratory bird population. In 1916, Canada and the United States joined forces through the Migratory Birds Convention, and the following year the Parliament signed the Migratory Birds Convention Act. This act made the management of certain migratory birds the responsibility of the federal government. In 1973, the Canada Wildlife Act allowed the government to con-duct wildlife research and coordinate wildlife conservation activ-ities with the various provinces.

The CWS works in conjunction with the USFWS and other organizations to maintain maximum populations of waterfowl. The North American Waterfowl Management Plan is a joint billion-dollar program of Canada and the United States to pro-tect wetland habitats in both countries.

The CWS works to protect all endangered species and has developed renewal, rehabilitation, and rescue programs. The CWS is also involved in international collaborations through the Latin America Program and the Western Hemisphere Shorebird Reserve Network. An information exchange program with the United States, Russia, Norway, and Denmark provides research on the polar bear. The CWS was also instrumental in the establishment of the National Wildlife Areas and Migratory Bird Sanctuaries, with more that 140 refuges in Canada.

The CWS also conducts research on the effects of chemical contamination of wildlife resulting from pesticides, acid rain, and toxins that enter ecosystems through agriculture, industry, and urbanization.

For job opportunities with the CWS, go to the website at www.cws-scf.ec.gc.ca or write to Canadian Wildlife Service, Environment Canada, Ottawa, Ontario, K1A 0H3.

State Jobs for Biological Scientists

Many states have rather stringent requirements for employment, including physical health, education, and experience. Be sure to check with your state agency for all those details before you apply. Government jobs are usually fairly stable, and the career track is clearly spelled out for you. On the other hand, they are also very competitive, so your education and training are very important.

Each state has a slightly different name for its conservation or wildlife agency. They vary from Department of Fish and Game to Division of Fisheries and Wildlife, Department of Natural Resources, Department of Natural Resources, or Environmental Conservation Division.

You can identify the agency by consulting your local telephone book under State Government, or you can find these agency listings on-line. The Public Service Employees Network, for example, can help you find agencies and job openings at www .pse-net.com/joblistings/joblisting.htm. Median annual earnings for biological scientists working for state governments, except in education and hospitals, is $38,000.

Private-Sector Jobs for Biological Scientists

Recruiting for many private-sector jobs starts with advertisements in the local newspaper or the newsletter or a professional organization. Organizations with branches throughout the country, such as Greenpeace, might advertise in the *Wall Street Journal*, the *New York Times*, or other appropriate national publications. Positions available at their headquarters are advertised in the local city newspapers.

The Sierra Club

The Sierra Club has a job hot line telephone number (415-977-5744) in San Francisco. The club has more than six hundred thousand members and its mission is

- to explore, enjoy, and protect the wild places of the Earth

- to practice and promote the responsible use of the Earth's ecosystems and resources

- to educate and enlist humanity to protect and restore the quality of the natural and human environment

- to use all lawful means to carry out these objectives

Founded in 1892 by John Muir, the Sierra Club is a leading grass-roots conservation organization. Each chapter of the Sierra Club handles its own recruitment and can be directly contacted for employment. These chapters are located in every state and also in Canada. Available positions are posted on its website at www.sierraclub.org. If you find a job on-line that appeals to you, send a hard copy of your resume to the Human Resources Department of the San Francisco headquarters. The Sierra Club also has a bookstore on its website that specializes in books on the environment.

Citizens for a Better Environment

This organization, founded in 1971, is an example of a regional environmental organization that serves a more limited area. With offices in Illinois, Wisconsin, and Minnesota, its stated mission is to safeguard human health by decreasing pollution; to enhance the environment where people live, work, and play; and to involve citizens in decisions that affect the health of their environment. Various programs involve many people from diverse backgrounds, including lawyers, scientists, engineers, and community organizers who develop strategies for improving environmental quality. An organization like this might be a good place to gain experience through volunteer work during your summer breaks from high school or college.

Choosing a Biology Career

So if you decide that your love of nature will lead you to the field of biology, whether as an aquatic, wildlife, or fisheries biologist, an ecologist or biotechnologist, your opportunities for employment are very favorable over the next several years. This is especially true in the fields of waste disposal, pollution, and disease control. Since our society is growing older, any biological problems associated with aging will have to be studied, along with associated diseases, drugs, and medicines.

If you want to become a biologist, you will have to take some very definite steps in preparing for your career. Careful thought concerning where you want to work, in which area of the biological sciences, and for whom you want to work will affect your decision. The choices are wide and various, and only you can set the limits of your achievement.

You already know of the environmental problems with water, air, and land. It is now up to you to do something lasting to preserve these natural resources that you love so much.

For Further Information

Associations

American Society for Microbiology
1752 N Street NW
Washington, DC 20035
www.asmusa.org

Botanical Society of America
1735 Neil Avenue
Columbus, OH 43210
www.botany.org

Centers for Disease Control
1600 Clifton Road
Atlanta, GA 30341
www.cdc.gov

Dow Chemical Company
2030 Dow Center
Midland, MI 48641
www.dow.com

Amgen
One Amgen Center Drive
Thousand Oaks, CA 91320
www.amgen.com

Biotechnology Industry Organization (BIO)
1625 K Street NW
Washington, DC 20006

American Association of Zoo Keepers
635 SW Gage Boulevard
Topeka, KS 66606
www.aazk.org

American Association of Zoo Veterinarians
6 North Pennell Road
Media, PA 19063

American Ornithologists' Union
c/o Division of Birds MRC116
National Museum of Natural History
Washington, DC 20560

American Zoo and Aquariums Association
AZA Executive Offices
8403 Colesville Road, Suite 710
Silver Spring, MD 20910
www.aza.org

National Audubon Society
700 Broadway
New York, NY 10003
www.audubon.org

National Association of Biology Teachers
12030 Sunrise Valley Drive
Reston, VA 20191
www.nabt.org

U. S. Department of the Interior
U.S. Fish and Wildlife Service
1849 C Street NW
Washington, DC 20240
www.fws.gov

The Sierra Club
85 Second Street, Second Floor
San Francisco, CA 94105
www.sierraclub.org

The Nature Conservancy
4545 Fairfax Drive
Arlington, VA 22203
www.tcn.org

The Wilderness Society
1615 M Street NW
Washington, DC 20036
www.wilderness.org

American Fisheries Society
5410 Grosvenor Lane
Bethesda, MD 20814
www.fisheries.org
   Publications: *North American Journal of Fisheries
   Management*, *North American Journal of Aquaculture*,
   Journal of Aquatic Animal Health, *Fisheries*

Wildlife Management Institute
1101 Fourteenth Street NW, Suite 801
Washington, DC 20005

University-National Oceanographic Laboratory System office
P.O. Box 392
Saunderstown, RI 02874

National Marine Fishery Service
1335 East West Highway
Silver Spring, MD 20910
www.nmfs.noaa.gov

Canadian Wildlife Service
Environment Canada
Ottawa, ON K1A 0H3
Canada
www.cws-scf.ec.gc.ca

Federal Research Service, Inc.
370 Maple Avenue W, Suite 5
Vienna, VA 22183
www.fedjobs.com

Federal Jobs Digest
www.jobsfed.com

Wildlife Information Center
P.O. Box 198
Slatington, PA 18080
www.wildlifeinfo.org

American Geophysical Union
2000 Florida Avenue NW
Washington, DC 20009
www.agu.org

Marine Technology Society Publications
18281 L Street NW, Suite 906
Washington, DC 20036
   Publications: *Ocean Opportunities Career Guide, University
   Curricula in Oceanography and Related Fields*

The Oceanography Society
5912 LeMay Road
Rockville, MD 20851
   Publications: *Careers in Oceanography and Marine-Related
   Fields, Oceanography*
www.tos.org

U.S. Department of Agriculture
Office of Personnel and Recruitment Division
Fourteenth and Indepence Avenue SW, Room 301W
Washington, DC 20250

National Fish and Wildlife Foundation
1120 Connecticut Avenue NW, Suite 900
Washington, DC 20036
www.nfwf.org

Publications

Basta, N. *The Environmental Career Guide*. John Wiley Press,
  1992.

Catchpole, C.K. and P.J. Slater. *Bird Song: Biological Themes
  and Variations*. Cambridge University Press, 1995.

Chronicle Guidance Publications, 66 Aurora Street, P.O. Box
  1190, Moravia, NY 13118:
  "Marine Biologists" (Career Brief 543)
  "Wildlife Biologists" (Career Brief 453)
  "Zookeepers" (Career Brief 288)
  "Zoologists" (Career Brief 237)

Corman, Dick. *Zoo Savers*. Dume Publishing, 1996.

National Audubon Society Book of Wild Birds. Wings Books,
  1997.

Nowak, Ronald M. *Walker's Primates of the World*. Johns
  Hopkins University Press, 1999.

*Peterson's Guide to Graduate Programs in the Biological and
  Agricultural Sciences*. Peterson's Guides, Inc. 1993.

CHAPTER THREE

Down on the Farm

The purpose of agriculture, or the science of producing crops and livestock, is to increase food production and protect the land from deterioration. In its early history, agriculture encouraged stable human settlements and was an economic and social organizational force. During the sixteenth and seventeenth centuries, crop and farming methods became more sophisticated, and in the nineteenth century, the invention of farm machines increased production. Modern agriculture methods involve the use of pesticides and fertilizers, refrigeration, and the creation of genetically engineered food. Agriculture affects all of us because it supplies us with one of our most fundamental needs: food. In this country, the food supply is abundant. Supermarkets overflow with a variety of nutritional foods.

Agriculture has historically been a powerful economic and social force in human life. However, the picture of the family farm with a big red barn, animals roaming freely, and acres devoted to life-sustaining crop production has recently undergone some radical changes. Because of a complicated series of events, more than 50 percent of farmers in the Midwest heartland have gone out of business. They have been largely superseded by agribusiness—huge conglomerates blamed by many for confining animals in small, overcrowded cages; widespread use of antibiotics and growth hormones; crops deluged with pesticides; and genetically engineered and irradiated food.

The changes in the past hundred years are the result of more efficient use of machinery, the increased sophistication of research techniques, corporate involvement in the food chain, and the availability of rapid global communication. For example, the incidence in "mad cow" disease in England triggered a general boycott of beef exports from that country. And some European countries will not import genetically engineered food from the United States. Scattered outbreaks of the *E. coli* virus in contaminated meat, the increased awareness of the hazards of pesticides, and uncertainties about the impact of genetic engineering and irradiation have led to the growing popularity of organically grown and processed meat, eggs, dairy products, fruits, and vegetables.

This is all part of an international concern for the health and safety of the food we eat. With the global proliferation of food franchises, such as McDonald's, people all over the world are more aware of the origins of the food they consume. Trade agreements with other countries involving food are challenged because of varying food policies of each country.

Some people demand the abolition of genetically engineered food; others want it labeled so that the consumer can make the choice. An estimated one-fourth of U.S. corn and one-third of U.S. soybeans are grown from genetically modified seeds. People worry about these food products introducing contamination to other species' food sources and the development of weeds that are immune to insecticides. People who are allergic to certain foods may not know whether genes from those foods have been spliced into a food product they are not allergic to.

The same concerns revolve around irradiated food, especially because there are no long-term studies available to the public. On a short-term basis, some studies have indicated a destruction of certain vitamins in irradiated meat, and the possible production of toxic or carcinogenic chemicals.

The U.S. Department of Agriculture (USDA) and the Food and Drug Administration (FDA) set the regulatory standards of food and drugs in this country. Since people are now more informed about what is happening in this field, new challenges and opportunities are "on the plate" for these agencies. Because consumers are concerned about pesticides, they have turned in growing numbers to foods labeled "organic," and the USDA has recently issued new and stricter guidelines for the use of that word. As people become more informed about how their food is produced, they will present both challenges and opportunities to all involved in the food chain. And it all goes back to agriculture—the science of the production of crops and livestock.

The Importance of Agronomists

Agronomy goes hand in hand with agriculture because it is concerned with soil management and the breeding, physiology, and production of crops. Major crops, such as cotton, soybeans, and wheat, are its chief concern.

What Agronomists Do

Much of the effort of today's agronomists is applied to reducing environmental pollution. Some agronomists may be primarily concerned with how pesticides react in the soil and groundwater. They investigate how long it takes for them to break down and how toxic the process will be. Others concentrate on the dumping of waste material into the soil.

Other agronomists, who want to work more closely with farming problems, work at agricultural extension services. These are usually located at land-grant universities, where agronomists work with specific problems of farmers and help them to manage their farms better. The federal government also employs agronomists in the Soil Conservation Service and the Forest Service. These agronomists' concerns are primarily with farmers and ranchers and how they can manage their land effectively and conserve the soil at the same time.

Many agronomists are increasingly becoming farmers and ranchers themselves. Their college or university education is actually utilized on their own crops and soil to make a living.

Since agronomists are involved in the vital work of crop production and soil conservation, their work is needed all over the world. Universities, government agencies, and various foundations, as well as agriculture-related businesses with branches in foreign countries, need the services of agronomists to help solve the nutritional needs of developing nations throughout the world. So if you are a person with a bit of wanderlust, you may consider agronomy as a career.

Educational Requirements

Now that your curiosity has been aroused, you might ask yourself how you might become an agronomist. In high school, you should study the basic sciences, including biology, chemistry, math, and physics. English is required, and foreign languages are recommended if you see yourself in a faraway place in the future.

When you get to college, the following courses are highly recommended: geology, botany, microbiology, genetics, plant physiology, soil chemistry, plant pathology, entomology; biochemistry, and meteorology. With the bachelor of science degree, you could be a farmer, agricultural agent, or soil conservationist.

If you decide to get a master's degree, you will find more career opportunities available, both in research and agricultural extension programs. Both governmental and private-sector agencies and organizations need highly skilled and educated professionals now and in the future as the need for environmentally safe crops and "clean" soil continues.

Other Types of Agriculture Careers

Agricultural Pest Control Specialists

If you are a nature lover interested in working on agricultural problems, but you don't want to devote as much time to your education as an agronomist, you may consider the career of agricultural pest control specialist. On the job, you would take samples of crops and inspect them for signs of dangerous organisms or harmful insect infestation. You would be able to assist in proposing effective methods of disease prevention or using predators to eradicate the offending pests.

The specialist often trains and coordinates crews of workers who are brought in to spray pesticides after they learn to operate the equipment and applicators. At this level, the specialist also has to use management skills to make assignments, train workers, evaluate them, and be responsible for the working order of all equipment.

Pest control specialists are responsible for working with farmers and governmental agencies. They may work on land or occasionally from airplanes, where they will apply pesticides from the air.

To be hired as a trainee, you should have two years of full-time agricultural work experience. Six months of these two years should be in agricultural pest control work. However, you may substitute one and one-half years of college course work for the agricultural work experience. As a pest control specialist, you will have to be knowledgeable about surveying and controlling pests as well as about the current laws and regulations regarding pesticides.

Your prospects for employment as a pest control specialist are quite good, primarily with state and federal government agencies. Some states now require licensing, so be sure to check with your state's licensing board. In order to be licensed, it will be necessary to have a college degree in many states, but you will have to keep up with the changing educational standards for licensing.

Pest Control Helpers

Those of you who want to enter the pest control field before committing to a great deal of education may want to start out as a pest control helper. As a helper, you would assist in controlling rodents in agricultural fields and buildings. You might set traps, dig out harmful weeds, burn or spray, and try to identify likely places of infestation.

To become a pest control helper, you will have to be healthy and strong, dexterous and agile. But there are no educational standards or work experience requirements for the job. You may then advance, with some work experience, to the title of pest exterminator.

Pest Exterminators

Pest exterminators are employed by private industry and are found in the city and on the farm. Pests can infest not only crops but also buildings and other farm facilities and even farm animals. After initial inspections, exterminators make recommendations for treatment. Since termites are often the major culprits in any wooden structure, inspectors and helpers repair damage to both the structure and the soil.

Much of your work as a pest exterminator will be outdoors in all kinds of weather conditions. It will be strenuous and may involve bending, crawling, climbing, and lifting. You will have to be physically strong and have stamina to do this kind of work.

Although there are no educational requirements for this work, some states require licensing. You will have to know about rules and regulations concerning pesticides; dangerous pests, and extermination and prevention methods. You generally become an exterminator by receiving on-the-job training as a helper.

Entomologists

Entomologists are divided into two categories: systematic and economic. Both work with insects. Systematic entomologists work in laboratories; economic, in the field. Economic entomologists determine the geographical range of insects through surveys, and then their economic impact is evaluated.

You can become an entomologist with a bachelor's degree with emphasis on entomology and the zoological sciences. You must know how to classify major pests and how to identify and control them. You should also be familiar with horticulture, plant relationships, and plant pests as they relate to agriculture.

Entomology Field Assistants

Working alongside entomologists are entomology field assistants, who aid in trapping, fumigating, and spraying insects. They also supervise work crews and keep records. Often their work includes writing reports about their fieldwork.

With some work experience, assistants can survey infestations, track insect populations, evaluate control programs, and measure results. As with most environmental workers, field assistants are called upon to work with other specialists and technicians in government agencies and agriculture-related businesses.

You will need at least two years of agriculture-related work to obtain an entry-level position as an entomology field assistant. Some of this experience should include work on insect control projects. You will have to know about pest control methods and equipment, which may include spray guns and turbine blowers. Your career will probably be with local and state government agencies, and you can work your way up with additional experience.

Plant Physiologists

Plant physiologists divide their work between the field and the laboratory. They conduct research on pesticides and then apply it to agricultural crops and plants. Plant physiologists also investigate the toxicity of pesticides and chemicals that are applied to agriculture.

If you work for the government, you may advise manufacturers about the safety of new pesticides before they are labeled. Or you may testify at public hearings or in court as an expert witness. As with other scientists working with the natural environment, you may work with other scientists, technicians, agriculture extension service workers, and various other professionals.

To be a plant physiologist, you have to have a college degree. You should study all the biological sciences with a major in plant physiology. You would then be qualified for an entry-level position if you have no work experience. The more work experience and education you have, the better chance you will have for increased responsibilities and salary. Your best career opportunities are now with state and local government.

The Pesticide Controversy

The use of pesticides has, of course, caused a great deal of controversy in recent years. Many that have been used in the past are considered too toxic for use now. They have, therefore, been banned. Some that are now used are being challenged by independent organizations as being carcinogenic or too toxic for use in the food chain. Federal, state, and local governments have set up regulatory agencies for toxins and pesticides, and private organizations serve a vital watchdog function to those agencies to protect the environment and plant, animal, and human life.

The Federal Insecticide, Fungicide, and Rodenticide Act of 1947 was amended in 1972 and revised in 1978. Essentially it provides for federal control over the application of pesticides and regulation of the marketing of these products. It has become apparent in recent years that protection of the environment is everybody's job and that particular attention has to be paid to any substance used on crops or in the soil that holds the crops.

For instance, a U.S. Geological Survey study found that pesticides commonly used on crops in Illinois were getting into the rainwater by evaporating into the clouds. As these clouds moved, the polluted rain could then fall in any location. The pesticides in question were atrazine, alachlor, and metolachlor. In some places where the rainwater had fallen, the concentration of pesticides exceeded the U.S. Environmental Protection Agency (EPA) standards. This may be why the now-banned DDT can still be found all over the world. This also demonstrates that environmental concerns are global and must be tackled both locally and globally. Government, industry, and private associations must continually monitor the natural environment and make their reports known to the public for its input.

The EPA acknowledges that the use of pesticides is a two-edged sword. Some pesticides have actually reduced crop damage; others have saved lives by controlling insects that carry diseases. They have helped to preserve forests and parks and have stopped fruit from dropping before it is ripe. They can also retard fungicidal growth.

But whenever they stay in the environment and spread beyond the area where they are intended to be of use, they may invade the food we eat, the air we breathe, and the land that sustains the food. They become dangerous and harmful. They may even be affecting the reproductive cycle of certain birds and the ability of species to survive.

Experts in agricultural entomology estimate that farmers have reduced the use of pesticides by 22 percent for soybeans and 16 percent for corn in Illinois alone. The trend for farmers may be to reduce the use of pesticides in general because they realize some of the dangers. It has also been estimated that the use of herbicides could be reduced by as much as 50 percent if farmers would alternate rows with weed-smothering crops or apply weed killer only where needed instead of on every crop.

Federal Agencies

The federal agencies set up to monitor toxic substances are the Environmental Protection Agency (EPA), the Food and Drug Administration (FDA), the Occupational Health and Safety Administration (OHSA), and the Consumer Product Safety Commission (CPSC). The EPA is primarily responsible for the protection of the environment from pesticides.

Agricultural Scientists

The work of agricultural scientists and technicians is with food production and processing; they may test crops for quality and yield, or they may test plants and animals for resistance to insects and disease. In so doing, they have to monitor experiments and evaluate results. Most of their work is done outdoors and is often dangerous since they may be working with toxic substances or diseased organisms.

Agricultural science biologists need a bachelor's degree with a biological science major. You will have to take at least ten semester hours in plant biology and ten in vertebrate biology. In addition, you will have to be knowledgeable in botany, zoology, and mammalogy; botanical and zoological classification; pest control methods; and agriculture-related pest problems.

You may also want to work in nurseries or seed fields where you'll study insects and plants and serve as consultant to agriculture businesses. Or you could work at border control stations, inspecting and advising on regulations relating to agricultural imports and exports. This can occur at the borders between counties, states, and countries.

Agricultural scientists are needed throughout the world, but here in the United States you might want to contact the U.S.

Department of Agriculture for employment opportunities. State and local governments are also good sources for jobs as well as agricultural experiment stations and agribusiness.

Median annual earnings of agricultural and food scientists were $42,340 in 1998, with the lowest 10 percent earning less than $24,200 and the highest 10 percent earning more than $79,820. Starting salaries decrease if you have no experience. Your job prospects are quite good for the next several years, with the need to replace retired persons in this field accounting for many more job openings than projected growth.

Veterinarians

Veterinarians are employed by the U.S. Department of Agriculture and the U.S. Food and Drug Administration. In some cases, when they are working in the agricultural sciences, they try to improve breeding and livestock management or study diseases and insects that affect farm animals, including poultry. Agriculture experiment stations at state universities also employ agricultural veterinarians.

The demand for veterinarians who specialize in the public health sector, which includes agriculture, seems to be growing because there is an increasing animal census and because breeding methods have improved. Salaries vary according to the location of a practice and work experience.

If you choose to work with farm animals, your work will involve preventive care, vaccinations, and consultation with the farmer on feeding and production issues. In some cases, you will have to take care of wounds and fractures and perform surgery. Birthing of animals and artificial insemination may also be part of your practice.

Your prospects for a job working with farm animals may be better than in a small-animal practice because most graduates prefer not to work in rural areas. You may also consider employment as a livestock inspector who checks for transmissable diseases and, when found, quarantines animals. You may also inspect meat, poultry, or egg products at slaughterhouses or test live animals and carcasses for disease.

A doctor of veterinary medicine (DVM) degree from an accredited college and a license are required to practice. Preveterinary course work will include forty-five to ninety undergraduate semester hours with an emphasis on the sciences. Veterinary colleges offer courses in organic chemistry, physics, biochemistry, and general biology. In order to be accepted to your veterinary college of choice, you may also have to submit your test scores from the Graduate Record Examination (GRE), the Veterinary College Admission Test (VCAT), or the Medical College Admission Test (MCAT). Formal or volunteer experience with farm animals will give you a leg up on the competition, which is very high. There are only twenty-seven accredited veterinary colleges in the United States.

If you live in Canada and you want to obtain a DVM degree, you must have a minimum of six years of university education with two years of preveterinary study in your undergraduate years. For more information about the veterinary profession in Canada, contact the Canadian Veterinarian Medical Association listed at the end of this chapter.

Chemists

If your specialty is chemistry, you can also become involved in agriculture. Because of the many pollutants in the environment, organic, inorganic, analytical, and physical chemists are needed to work in connection with governmental agencies and other agricultural scientists. You will probably divide your work between the field and the laboratory, primarily helping to enforce the laws that ensure safety in the manufacture of chemicals used in agriculture. In the laboratory, you will examine pesticides, analyze them and see if they are toxic. Then you will determine under which conditions and dosages they pollute or contaminate. You will have to collect samples in the field and then follow certain scientific procedures to evaluate solutions. In your analysis and evaluation, you will deal with pesticides, fertilizers, residues, and feed. Since your work directly involves public health, you may be called on to present your findings at public hearings and evaluate the environmental impact of pesticides and chemicals.

You will need a degree in chemistry or biochemistry. Work experience of one or two years may also may be required for some jobs if you don't have a master's or doctoral degree. You will find employment with the government or industry. Your job title may be either agricultural chemist or environmental chemist. Salaries vary according to academic degree, work experience, and private- or public-sector employment.

Chemical Technicians

Chemical technicians work alongside chemists in the manufacturing process or on the farm. They should have a background in applied chemistry, mathematics, and basic laboratory equipment. These skills can be acquired at an accredited college or in a two-year program. Junior or community colleges, some trade or technical schools, and four-year colleges will offer you the necessary courses.

You may get further training on the job, but employers are increasingly looking for technicians with a two-year degree rather than unskilled workers who have to be completely trained on the job. Other chemical technicians have a bachelor's degree in chemistry or have taken several science and math courses at a four-year college. Median hourly earnings for chemical technicians in 1998 were $15.30.

Biotechnologists

Biotechnologists are also needed in agriculture and pesticide work. Biotechnology applies the disciplines of biochemistry,

chemistry, microbiology, and chemical engineering to a wide variety of products and processes. Biotechnologists investigate ways to improve crops through alteration of genes so that plants manufacture their own natural pesticides. They also work on producing plants with more protein in the hope of improving their nutritional value.

The Need for Agricultural Professionals

We can now understand, from viewing these career possibilities, that planting food and bringing it to harvest, guaranteeing the health of plants and animals, and using the soil wisely is a very complex operation. Growing plants and animals depends on clean air, suitable soil, nonpolluted water, and nutritional feed and fertilizers. Farming in this country no longer resembles a Norman Rockwell illustration of a nuclear family tilling the soil on its own plot of land that has been passed on from generation to generation. Pollution, advanced technology, agribusiness, and harmful pesticides and chemicals have made dealing with the food chain very complicated. Many farmers have opted for organic methods in order to completely avoid the hazards of applying any pesticide to crops.

In an area as vital as agriculture, it is essential that all scientists and technicians work together with the farmer, rancher, consumer, and government agencies to provide safe food today and improved crops for tomorrow. Our country and the world's population are in great need of good food and an equitable distribution of it.

Highly educated and trained professionals are needed. They should be knowledgeable in their field and should have some familiarity with computers, satellites, and telemetry instruments. Interdisciplinary cooperation and application of mathematics, communication skills, social sciences, critical thinking, and analytical skills will have to be utilized to make it all happen. Laboratory workers will have to share with field workers, chemists with biologists, biotechnologists with agronomists, soil scientists with pest control specialists. Plant and animal physiologists will share information with ecologists and crop specialists; and state, local, and federal agencies will have to enforce laws concerning labeling and use of agricultural products. Consumers will have to be aware of the ramifications of all these processes and demand the safety and nutrition of all foods that are consumed by animals and humans. Creative solutions will have to be found for the problems of world hunger.

Agricultural Organizations

Farm Animal Reform Movement

For every government agency or industry involved with agriculture, there are as many independent agencies seeking protection of animals on factory farms and in agribusiness. One such organization is the Farm Animal Reform Movement (FARM). The organization sponsors the annual Great American Meatout, when Americans are urged not to eat meat for one day. By protesting slaughterhouse practices and factory farming of chickens and cattle and supporting the Veal Calf Protection Act of 1990, this group is doing a great deal toward effecting more humane treatment of farm animals.

Humane Farming Association

Another organization is the Humane Farming Association, well known for the campaign against factory farming and its effects on the quality of meat produced. Its campaign to boycott veal is carried out through TV commercials, education, and legislation.

Although these organizations may not have many career opportunities, they will provide you with information about the farming industry that you might not get from more traditional agencies.

So the future should be bright, complex, exciting, and rewarding for you if you choose to show your love of nature in the very important field of agriculture. No matter which path you take, education, training, willingness to work with others to come up with solutions, eagerness to learn new techniques, and the ability to devise new strategies will help you find a career. You may work in the private or public sector or buy your own farm or ranch and apply your knowledge and ideas to your own plot of land.

For Further Information

Associations

American Society of Agronomy
Crop Science Society of America
Soil Science Society of America
677 South Segoe Road
Madison, WI 53711
www.agronomy.org

Entomological Society of America
9301 Annapolis Road
Lanham, MD 20706
www.entsoc.org

Food and Agricultural Careers for Tomorrow
Purdue University
1140 Agricultural Administration Building
West Lafayette, IN 47907

Institute of Food Technologists
221 North La Salle Street, Suite 300
Chicago, IL 60601
www.ift.org

American Veterinary Medical Association
1931 North Meacham Road, Suite 100
Schaumburg, IL 60173
www.avma.org

Association of American Veterinary Medical Colleges and
National Association of Federal Veterinarians
1101 Vermont Avenue NW, Suite 710
Washington, DC 20005
http://aavmc.org

CHAPTER FOUR

Planning the Land for Use

The word "land" probably means something different to everyone. It can mean the ground, earth, or soil from which we receive nourishment. It can mean grassland, pasture, and meadow for plant growth, or sand for desert and beach. It means something solid underfoot and something on which we build our homes and businesses. It is part of our everyday life in many ways, and if we have any respect for it in all its meanings and dimensions, we have to plan its use carefully. Too many species are dependent on fertile, verdant, and unpolluted land for survival for anyone to take the care of it lightly.

Since all natural resources are finite, many people have taken responsible positions to ensure that the land is used appropriately, allowing for the survival of all the species that are dependent on it.

Preserving the Earth

Are there gaps in our care and feeding of the great Mother Earth? Many would answer "yes," and those people are probably actively employed in providing for the proper use of the land. The land is simply not infinite; natural resources can be depleted if they are not carefully utilized and conserved. The soil can be contaminated, making it useless for growing or grazing. The plants and animals that are dependent on the earth for sustenance and, indeed, existence are in danger of extinction if their natural habitats are destroyed, and the extinction of any species upsets the ecological balance. For just as biologists, geologists, chemists and other environmental professionals must work together to ensure a healthy and wholesome life for all living things, all natural organisms are interdependent and must function as a team to survive.

Wildlife, farm animals, birds, plants, flowers, trees, and humans all depend on the earth for existence. But for too long we have abused the earth, thinking that it would always be there for our use. Or perhaps we weren't thinking at all. We became careless, we developed selfish interests in the use of the land, we forgot how important it is to us and future generations. There is no hidden or secret planet that can support life systems as we know them. So we have to take some serious steps to use the land that we still have appropriately, to consider all requests for its use, and to work toward an equitable solution for its proper utilization.

Protective Laws and Government Agencies

We do have local and federal laws that will help us maintain public lands and some governmental agencies that are charged with protecting and preserving land-based natural resources. The Department of Interior's U.S. Geological Survey, the National Park Service, Bureau of Land Management, and Bureau of Reclamation all have responsibilities and, therefore, employment possibilities for people who are interested in land use and planning. The Forest Service of the Department of Agriculture, as well as municipal and state governments, employs land planners, landscape architects, surveyors, landscape designers, and plant scientists.

The Federal Highway Administration

The Federal Highway Administration ensures the safety and efficiency of U.S. highways, overseeing policy, planning, research, design, construction, and maintenance of the highway transportation system. It also administers the Federal Lands Highway Program that oversees the survey, design, and construction of federal highways and roads in forests, Native American reservations, and defense access roads. The Federal Lands Highway Program supplies engineering services to plan, design, construct, and rehabilitate highways and bridges that access federally owned lands.

The Highway Administration has cooperative agreements with the National Park Service and the Bureau of Indian Affairs to coordinate programs and funding for more than eighty thousand miles of federally owned roads. It employs about six hundred workers in Washington, D.C.; Sterling, Virginia; Denver, Colorado; and Vancouver, Washington.

Other partnerships include the Bureau of Land Management, Federal Aviation Administration, National Park Service, U.S. Army Corps of Engineers, U.S. Forest Service, U.S. Department of Transportation, and state and local governments.

The National Park and Forest Service

The National Park and Forest Services have been around since the beginning of the twentieth century, but increased awareness of the general environment occurred in the 1970s when laws were passed and agencies established to set and enforce standards. The National Environmental Policy Act provides for environmental impact statements for any project that will affect human life. The Endangered Species Act and the Federal Surface Mining and Reclamation Act of 1977 were also established during that time.

The Environmental Protection Agency

The Environmental Protection Agency (EPA) was established in 1970 by merging several other departments and agencies. The idea was to have a unified national program to solve environmental problems rather than rely on a wide variety of local ordinances throughout the country. The EPA is involved with these environmental concerns: air, water, pesticides, noise, drinking water, solid waste, toxic substances, and radiation. It is responsible for policy, standards, support, and evaluation of environmental factors through its regional offices. The EPA is also responsible for enforcing all laws concerning the environment.

The National Environmental Policy Act

In 1970, the National Environmental Policy Act (NEPA) became law. It was meant to establish a balance between human needs and the natural environment. Because of the NEPA, the Council on Environmental Quality was conceived to help the president determine sound environmental policy on a national basis. This council makes it necessary for all federal agencies to prepare environmental impact statements before they begin any major project, including construction of nuclear power plants, highways, and bridges.

A draft of all possibilities and ramifications is then given to federal, state, and local agencies for review and approval. After every responsible jurisdiction has commented on, objected to, revised, and resolved the problems, the EPA receives a copy, which then becomes available to the public.

These statements are extremely detailed and include probable and indirect ramifications on the ecology of a given area, short-term and long-term evaluations, and any possibilities of irretrievable damage to all aspects of the environment. And although the EPA cannot legally prevent another federal agency from going ahead with a project, it has the responsibility to advise the other agencies and the public of the environmental consequences.

These environmental impact statements can be crucial to land planners and architects. Further legislation that also affects these workers are the Coastal Zone Management Act, the Resource Conservation and Recovery Act of 1976, the Clean Air Act, and the Safe Drinking Water Act.

Land Planners

Because the land in all its various forms is used for many purposes, land planners are needed for city and regional planning, residential subdivisions, rural areas, parks, and forests. Highways and housing developments, shopping malls and golf courses, airports and recreation areas—all require the work of the land planner.

Site planning involves collaborations with architects, engineers, surveyors, and environmental specialists to develop commercial, residential, recreational, and industrial projects. Natural land planning involves environmental engineers, forest managers, and wildlife biologists. Wildlife, plants, and nature trails may be designed into a development through the skilled use of a planning team. Civil engineers, surveyors, and landscape architects work with environmental specialists for stormwater management, road design, and erosion control.

What Land Planners Do

Planners have to know about local zoning regulations, pollution control laws, and building codes. Projects have to be approved by utility companies, zoning agencies, and city, state, and federal agencies to obtrain permits for planned development. Planners are responsible for taking in all points of view, such as the real estate developer, the historic preservation professional, the engineers and technicians, and the local citizenry, and come up with a plan that is environmentally harmonious and balanced. Besides land issues, air and water safety must also be considered. In addition to all these factors, economic and social problems are part of the mix that the land planner has to deal with.

After initial discussions with the concerned parties, land planners study analyses of the soil, water, and air as well as any other natural resources that will be affected by the project. These may include plants, wildlife, insects, trees, rivers, and lakes.

The land planner also has to consider the goals of the project at this stage. For example, the goals of rehabilitating an urban neighborhood would be different from those of constructing an interstate highway. The land surrounding that under consideration will also have to be investigated.

When all factors have been thoroughly studied, the land planner has to make proposals and recommendations for the wisest use of the land, based on function, environmental requirements, and cost. All this information is entered into a computer and analyzed with whatever technical data is needed until the final report is completed. Then these recommendations are made known to governmental agencies, other involved professionals, and the general public for review.

Educational Requirements

Land planners work with diverse populations using a wide variety of skills, including analysis, communication, diplomacy, and sometimes economics. If you decide to become a land planner, you can take a couple of possible routes. You may prepare yourself during college, or you may combine education and work experience. At any rate, you should definitely plan an educational track that includes a master's degree.

If you are now in high school, you should begin to anticipate your undergraduate course work. Your major could be in planning, environmental studies, or urban studies. Your curriculum should include civil engineering, public administration, landscape architecture, natural science, and public health. Some social sciences such as economics, political science or law, geography, and a strong base in both oral and written communications should round out your college studies. You should also try to develop strong decision-making and problem-solving skills as well as critical-thinking abilities. With this combination, you will be prepared to pursue your master's degree in planning.

If you have the opportunity during your summer breaks, it would be a good idea to get a job at the planning department in your hometown, to attend public hearings on land-use projects, to volunteer at your local zoning board, or to work on a neighborhood rehabilitation project.

If you already have your undergraduate degree and are working in a related field, you still need a master's degree, and it would also be a good idea to get some work experience in law, zoning, geography, resource economics, or urban planning.

Finding a Job

As you begin your job search, you may want to take a geographic approach; that is, find out where the jobs are and be willing to relocate in order to start your career. This approach might increase your chances of finding what you want. However, because of the need for land planners, you may very well be able to stay where you are and find a job with your local government, historic preservation group, or consulting group. If you work in a small town, you may be required to do everything—that is, take the project from beginning to end. In a larger city, you may be more specialized and departmentalized and work under the instruction and supervision of a more experienced planner.

The recognized professional organization for land planners is the American Planning Association. Members are entitled to a job-listing service and publications on salary trends. Salaries, of course, will vary from state to state and agency to agency, but your entry-level salary with a master's degree should be about $26,000 a year.

Land planning seems to offer a rather bright future for people who are creative, analytical, proficient in communications skills, well versed in public policy and legislation, and dedicated to the goal of achieving environmental harmony and balance between humans, animals, and plants and the aesthetic and economic needs of the community.

Landscape Architects

Working closely with the land planner is the landscape architect. The American Society of Landscape Architecture states that there are about twenty-five thousand landscape architects now working in the United States in both the public and private sectors, universities, community services, and research.

Landscape architects play a vital role in the preservation of the environment by designing, planning, and managing the land. They are concerned not only with the beauty of the design but also with environmental impact and the best use of the land.

What Landscape Architects Do

Much like land planners, landscape architects work in urban, suburban, and rural settings, in parks, housing developments, national forests, or for a regional project encompassing a very large area. They must be able to solve problems, work with other professionals and community groups, speak and write English well, be proficient in graphic design, and have a deep commitment to the environment.

Landscape architects have to know about soil erosion, plant and animal relationships, and noise-absorbing vegetation. They usually work a great deal of the time on a site where a recreational facility, airport, highway, subdivision, industrial park, or shopping mall will be located. They may work for the municipal planning agency, a national park or forest, consulting firm, or developer. They work with planners, engineers, architects, and natural scientists, such as plant and animal physiologists.

In the process of their on-site analysis, they have to study the geography, topography, climate, and position of existing structures, such as buildings or bridges. Then they have to work on sketches, specifications, and budgetary requirements and eventually build an actual working model of the project. All details, such as roadways, parking facilities, walls, and fences, must be included on this model.

Their communication skills play a role because they have to prepare written reports, usually with detailed graphics, and make oral presentations on the feasibility of a particular project. Creativity, as well as highly developed technical skills, are needed at this stage of the process.

Educational Requirements

If you were the one in the family who liked to do the yard work, mow the lawn, plant the flower and vegetable gardens, trim the bushes, and prune the trees, you may be perfect for this line of work. But in addition to this basic aptitude, you will need a minimum of a college degree and, in some cases, a master's degree to become a landscape architect. An internship is often preferred by many employers.

As an undergraduate, you will be taking natural and social sciences, behavioral sciences, art, mathematics, surveying, landscape design and construction, landscape ecology, site design, and urban and rural planning. You may also study plant and soil science, geology, and general management. Courses in the environment are also available. English, math, and physical science courses and work in a design studio are also offered. You will probably be assigned to projects that will give you experience in computer-aided design (CAD) and video simulations. The bachelor's degree could take four or five years.

A master's degree or doctorate is necessary if you want to be a university lecturer or engage in specialized research. For the master's degree, you have two choices: a professional three-year program for those with a bachelor's degree in another field, or a professional degree, which is a two-year program with a bachelor's degree in landscape architecture.

Determine whether your state requires a license in addition to your degree in order to practice. This usually consists of passing an examination and may also include some supervised practice.

The accreditating agencies for programs in landscape architecture are the Landscape Architectural Accreditation Board of the American Society of Landscape Architects (ASLA) and the Canadian Society of Landscape Architects Accredititation Council (CSLAAC). Nearly sixty universities in both countries offer forty-six accredited undergraduate and twenty-nine postgraduate programs. Forty-six states require licenses that are based on the Landscape Architect Registration Examination (LARE). In order to be licensed, you will have to know about laws and environmental regulations, as well as about plants and soil indigenous to the particular state. State requirements vary, so it may be difficult to transfer your registration from state to state. Federal agencies do not require licensing. The ASLA website, www.asla.org, has on-line resources, including a bookstore, salary surverys, and a "joblink."

Types of Employment

Many landscape architects are self-employed or work for small firms. Therefore, benefits may not be generous. Others work in architectural and engineering firms or with the government. The federal government's primary employers of landscape architects are the Departments of Agriculture, Defense, and Interior, the Forest Service, and the National Park Service. The latter two have experienced some budget cuts recently and have contracted work out to private firms, opening up new employment opportunities. Your work as a landscape architect will be done in the office or at the worksite, and your hours will be fairly regular unless a deadline imposes some overtime.

After you have had several years' experience, you may become a project manager, associate, or partner. Salaries vary according to your experience and your employer, whether private or governmental. In the private sector, landscape architects had median annual earnings in 1998 of $37,930. The lowest 10 percent earned less than $22,800, and the highest 10 percent earned more than $78,920. In 1999, the average annual salary for all landscape architects in the federal government was about $57,500.

Careers Related to Land Planning

As you can see, land planning, design, and management are only possible when various dedicated professionals share information; analyze data; and make wise, safe, and healthy decisions based on ecological systems. For example, the land planner works with the realty specialist, who investigates all aspects of selling or leasing land, arranges for permits, and submits studies on the proper use of the land. Realty specialists may work with geologists, who have mapped the area that is being considered for use. The geologist uses maps that show minerals and bedrock in the area being considered for use and analyzes data collected from the actual site. They may all work with a cartographer, who designs maps of a specific area from aerial photos and other larger maps. All of these professionals are dependent on the work of the surveyor, who must be aware of the boundaries within which the project is to be constructed. With the help of surveyors, property disputes are avoided or ironed out based on titles and legal claims to the land.

Geographers

Geographers, who are versed in both the natural and social sciences, are being called on more and more for their expertise in land-use problems. They study not only the location of natural phenomena but also the reason for that location. They analyze both physical and cultural aspects with emphasis on interpreting the ever-changing environment.

Geographers are employed by government and private agencies to research urban renewal, resource management, and highway systems. Sophisticated techniques used by contemporary geographers include remote sensing and statistical analyses to promote wise land use.

Those geographers who specialize in landforms and soil erosion may be called on to help in city planning or regional planning where geographic considerations are at stake. Geographers are uniquely qualified to study human relationships in regard to their physical environment.

If you are interested in becoming a geographer, see if you have the following characteristics:

- You like to study maps.

- You are curious about places and foreign countries.

- You like to work outside.

- You are a problem solver.

- You are technologically grounded.

- You want to make a connection between human life and the natural environment.

If you study geography, you might work as a cartographer, land officer, consulting biologist, environmental engineer, planner, or soil conservationist. Private businesses employ geographers to help them locate new industrial sites or plan transportation systems. City and county planners employ geographers in growing numbers because they often determine environmental considerations and risks.

Professional geographers need a bachelor's degree in geography, with emphasis on statistical methods, computers, cartography, communication skills, foreign language, environmental studies, field techniques, meteorology, climatology, and map design and interpretation. Additional course work might include oceanography, human geography, geomorphology, and environmental geography.

If you desire a better paying job, you should consider obtaining a master's degree, which will include an internship plus thirty to thirty-six semester or forty-five to fifty-four quarter hours. The entry-level salary range for the federal government is about $20,600 to $26,000 annually. If you hold a master's degree, you could expect to earn a salary starting at $31,200, and if you have a doctorate, you could start out earning $37,300.

The federal government employs geographers at the Defense Mapping Agency, the Bureau of the Census, and the U.S. Geological Survey (USGS). The USGS's website, www.mapping .usgs.gov, lists publications, posters, and CD-ROMs that may help with your job search.

The professional organization for geographers is the Association of American Geographers. Membership includes annual meetings, journals, and a newsletter as well as special publications and job listings.

Geographic Information System (GIS) Specialist

Many land-use professionals use a computer hardware and software system that stores, displays, analyzes, and maps information. Geographers, land planners, and government officials use the GIS to evaluate transportation systems, traffic, environmental problems, soil, and flood zones so that they can make the right decisions. You might also like to work with the Department of Agriculture, Department of Defense, the State Department, or the Central Intelligence Agency to interpret photos as a remote-sensing analyst.

Cartographers

Cartographers design, compile, and reproduce maps. Charting maps of land areas is done either manually or digitally. The federal government needs people to fill all these job categories through the Bureau of Land Management or the U.S. Geological Survey, both units of the Department of the Interior. At the GS-5 level, you would need a bachelor's degree or a combination of education (thirty semester hours in cartography) and related work experience. If you want to qualify with your bachelor's degree alone, you need at least thirty semester hours of cartography, related physical science, computer science, or physical geography. In addition, you would have to have at least six semester hours of scientific math. If you choose to work for the government, you may also find career opportunities at the Bureau of the Census, the Defense Mapping Agency, Federal Highway Administration, U.S. Army Corps of Engineers, U.S. Forest Service, or the Tennessee Valley Authority.

To prepare for a career in cartography, you would take college courses in principles of cartography, remote sensing, computer mapping, principles of map design, and geographic information systems (GIS). You would also learn to draw, read, and interpret maps. Although you need to learn hand-drawing techniques, most of today's cartographers work with sophisticated computer software. In addition to a bachelor's degree, a good internship and membership in a professional association can help you get started in your career.

Working to Nurture the Land

These are some of the careers available to you if you want to work on planning, designing, preserving, and understanding the land and its relationship to human needs and nature's ecological demands. The land is vast, natural, inspiring, life giving, fertile, and peaceful. But we have to work to keep it that way. It is not infinite; it must be nurtured, cared for, and used carefully and wisely so that future generations will be able to enjoy its physical beauty and spiritual benefits. Natural beauty can be cultivated and enhanced. It can be saved from further destruction and can provide recreational space for millions.

Municipal planners know that our natural resources can be safe havens for the many residents who are so used to concrete, brick, glass, and steel as their everyday environment. Parks, gardens, and green spaces can be incorporated into all new and existing city plans for rejuvenation and rehabilitation of the urban environment. Even when new buildings must be built, the total natural environment must not be destroyed to accommodate them. Planners and architects must know how to coordinate human needs with the needs of other species that are also dependent on the land for survival.

Technicians are responsible for preserving and maintaining the land; geologists, geographers, surveyors, and cartographers are called on for resource development, often for larger regional projects that are frequently sponsored by the federal government. Understanding the land and its various functions, plotting it for possible use, understanding interrelationships, and interpreting pertinent data are some of their responsibilities. All work closely with land planners and landscape architects.

So if the land is your passion, you will have various opportunities to plan and preserve it with these careers. If you are creative and appreciate the many facets of human life and the diversity of other species, land planning and architecture may be where you'll fit into an environmental career.

You'll now have to decide which career path interests you most, how much time you want to devote to education and training, and maybe even how much physical work you may want to do. Some of these jobs involve working closely with others from different areas of expertise; some require supervisory skills. Others rely more on physical strength.

Many of these career opportunities are available through municipal, state, and federal governmental agencies. However, many private associations and organizations, although they may not have a large staff of employees, are good sources of information about specific areas of land preservation. You may wish to contact them to help you get started in your career search. They may also have volunteer programs on a limited basis.

Whichever career you choose, you will know that you are playing a vital role in the preservation of the beauties of the earth and all life forms dependent on it. And you will help to bring about a more beautiful environment for generations to come.

For Further Information

Associations

American Geological Institute
4220 King Street
Alexandria, VA 22302
   Publication: *Careers in the Geosciences*

American Society of Landscape Architects
Career Information
636 Eye Street NW
Washington, DC 20001
www.asla.org

Canadian Society of Landscape Architects
P.O. Box 870
Station B
Ottawa, ON K1P 5P9
Canada
www.csla.ca

Association of American Geographers
1710 Sixteenth Street NW
Washington, DC 20009
www.aag.org

U.S. Geological Survey
Headquarters
John W. Powell Federal Building
12201 Sunrise Valley Drive
Reston, VA 20192
www.usgs.org

CHAPTER FIVE

Taking Care of the Forests and Other Natural Resources

*L*and planners and landscape architects, geographers and geologists, agronomists and plant physiologists, botanists and ecologists—all tend to the needs of the earth and the demands of human life. We'll see, as we explore the various career opportunities for nature lovers, that other professionals take care of the land, water, air, plants, and animals in a number of different ways.

We might also note here that the conservation and preservation of natural resources is a multidimensional and integrated search for solutions to the many problems of stewardship. So a biologist may work in a zoo or a forest; a geologist may study oceans, space, or earthquakes. A botanist could be employed on a farm, in a university setting, or in a park.

A full complement of environmental professionals—all of them concerned with some aspect of environmental safety and human need—could be working in a city park or national forest, a rural development or a suburban industrial site.

Forests: A Valuable Resource

The forests of our nation and the world are always in need of special care because they have one of the most important natural resources—trees. As well as trees, many other life forms depend on the natural ecological balance of the forest. Coexisting in the forest are grass, soil, rocks, air, water, wildlife, plants, and minerals—all participate in complex interrelationships. The National Forest Service manages 191 million acres of forest land, and there are more than 700 million acres of forest land outside that system, so many people with diverse skills are needed to make sure that our forests are well maintained.

Different types of forests include municipal, county, community, and federal parks; rangelands and wildlife sanctuaries; swampland; watersheds; and timberland and wilderness areas. Some of these areas are used for recreation; others, for habitat restoration. Some are used for logging; others, for wildlife protection. Some are used for cattle grazing; others, for animal rehabilitation.

There seems to be a growing awareness of the interrelatedness or holism of the forests and the life forms they conserve and protect. Those who work in forests and parks are truly resource managers because these lands must be protected from exploitation and unscrupulous development.

Preserving Forests

Both independent and government organizations and agencies are working, sometimes together, sometimes at odds with each other, to effectively manage, preserve, and restore the land and its resources. Private, state, and national forests may serve several purposes—recreational, industrial, and environmental—and sometimes these purposes do not coincide. For example, the paper industry needs wood from the trees in the forest, but trees remove carbon dioxide from the air and reduce the chance of global warming. Trees are also natural habitats for various species of wildlife and birds, such as the spotted owl. So conflicts arise between the human need for employment and paper, which the logging industry provides, and the growing awareness among private citizen groups of the importance of preserving the precious balance of nature. The Sierra Club's End Commercial Logging in Our National Forests campaign, for example, claims that the timber industry has turned our forests into clear-cuts and logging roads. (See Chapter 2 for a more detailed description of the Sierra Club.)

Human recreational activities in parks and forests may also have harmful effects on the diverse life forms there. This may cause friction between sportspeople, athletes, and campers, who wish to use the facilities and natural resources of the forest, and the independent environmental groups that carefully monitor habitat destruction, endangerment of species, and waste of resources.

When governmental agencies that are charged with steward-ship of public lands engage in practices that will adversely affect the life of various species in parks or forests, environmentally oriented organizations protest the action. When land developers or oil companies threaten animal or plant habitats, they can also expect vociferous protest from these same organizations.

Much research is being done regarding the necessity of tropical rain forests in the preservation of vital ecosystems. Still more research has to be done on forests and trees to see what effect they have on the total environment. However, many companies and industries are beginning to use recycled paper products so that fewer trees will have to be cut and less garbage will be produced and disposed of.

Careers in Forest Conservation

Passions run high when it comes to natural resource manage-ment and preservation, especially considering how many millions of acres are involved. And when you choose a career in conservation of parks or forests, you should think about whether you want to work for a governmental agency that has to follow the policy of the current administration or for an independent, grassroots organization that targets a specific species or devotes itself to playing the watchdog role for a variety of environmental issues. Whichever path you choose, commitment, education, endurance, skill, creativity, training, knowledge of the law, and sometimes physical strength will determine your career path.

Federal Government Jobs in Forestry

The National Forest Service (NFS), part of the Department of Agriculture (DOA), employs about thirty thousand permanent employees and fifteen thousand temporary employees. Among these are seven thousand forest technicians and five thousand foresters. In the 1960s and 1970s, the service created many new positions, including wildlife biologist, landscape architect, land management planner, and soil conservationist. In the 1980s and early 1990s, it expanded further by adding positions in law enforcement, recreation, planning, and conservation. Since then, it has reduced its workforce for more efficient operation and because the timber program was reduced.

The state and private forestry agencies partner with managers of private and state-run forests to ensure that more than seven hundred million acres of forest land are protected and well managed. This is achieved through beautification, fire prevention, and forest health protection programs. The NFS provides technical and financial assistance to agencies within the forestry community.

The research branch of the NFS employs more than twenty thousand workers. Its research scientists work in universities, laboratories, and stations all over the United States and study tree improvement; forest protection from fire, diseases, and pests; wilderness management; forest engineering; and urban forestry, among others.

We're going to look at some of the careers that are listed in the technical category. Included in the technical category are biologists, foresters, and engineers and their technicians. In each of these fields, people who operate and repair equipment and maintain machines are needed. And many of the same careers that we have already looked at, such as biologist, botanist, landscape architect, land planner, soil scientist, and plant physiologist, may turn up here or in the parks of this country. We'll also take a look at how they, along with ornithologists and animal rehabilitators, might function in a forest or park.

Foresters

What Foresters Do

Forests are probably best known for trees, but they also provide recreational opportunities and wildlife habitat. So foresters manage these areas in a variety of ways. In private lands, they may deal more with negotiating timber sales by working with loggers and pulpwood cutters. They have to balance the economic and recreational purposes with the environmental impact on ecosystems within the forest. They have to determine how to preserve habitats, water quality, and soil stability in order to conform to environmental standards and regulations. Among the duties of the forester in the state or federal systems are the management of public forests and the design of campgrounds and other recreational areas.

If lumber is a major product of the forest, foresters have to know the size of the trees and how much lumber the trees can yield. When foresters decide which trees are to be cut, they also have to decide which trees will replace them. If there is a forest fire, it may be necessary to replace a large section of the forest.

As a forester, you may also be able to choose a specialty, such as research, fire prevention, disease control, soil erosion, or logging practices. In addition to very specific knowledge about forest ecology, foresters have to supervise and train other workers, know all the laws and enforce them, travel when necessary, and react quickly to emergencies.

Qualifications

You will need a bachelor's degree in forestry and some practical experience to become a forester. Field trips and camps sponsored by forestry schools will give you a feel for this type of work. Or you can use your summer breaks to work in a city or state park or forest or volunteer witht a grassroots environmental group. Some colleges may accept this work as part of your credits.

In addition to your forestry courses, you will have to have highly developed oral and written communication skills, mathematics, biometrics, and computer knowledge. If you choose to specialize in a particular field or to engage in research, you will have to have an advanced degree. Specialties include wildlife conservation, entomology, genetics, tree culture, wood technology, or recreation.

Where to Find Jobs

Other federal agencies employing foresters are the Bureau of Land Management, the National Park Service, the Bureau of Indian Affairs, and the Tennessee Valley Authority. Every state has some agency concerned with forests, parks, and conservation that will provide career opportunities for foresters. Urban forestry, which involves tree planting in city parks and streets, is a new field with growing possibilities, and private consulting firms as well as grassroots environmental groups hire foresters.

The Society of American Foresters is a professional scientific and educational organization that is an advocate of professional forest management with certification programs for foresters and forest technicians.

The Canadian Forest Service has much the same mission as our National Forest Service, and Parks Canada is the equivalent to the National Park Service in the United States. The Canadian Institute of Forestry also works for the proper stewardship of Canadian forests by setting professional standards; attending national conferences; and conducting field trips, scientific presentations, and public speaking engagements. It has approximately twenty-four hundred members in twenty-three sections in Canada. Its members include scientists, foresters, technicians, technologists, and scientists.

So, as you can see, opportunities for foresters exist in national, state, and private forests and in cities, industry, and independent organizations. You may choose to become a forest technician or work in a nursery for a while before committing to the additional educational requirements of foresters.

Forest Technicians

What Forest Technicians Do

The forest technician's work in forests and parks is of vital necessity to the proper use of the land. Much of your work will have to do with patrolling the land, preserving it from ravaging fires, and protecting trees and the life forms dependent on them.

As a forest technician, you would be called on to assist foresters in planting trees, preventing fires, and constructing roads. One type of technician is the surveyor, who maps out where roads will be built. Other technicians are responsible for the health of the trees, so they inspect for harmful insects and diseases; prune or destroy trees when necessary; and pollinate, graft, and gather seeds under the supervision of the forester or plant scientist.

You may need supervisory skills if you oversee work crews for road building and repair, planting trees, and fighting fires. Some map interpretation and data collecting as well as report writing may be part of your job. Many tools are required to keep parks and forests in good condition, and you may have to use and repair them. You may also have to maintain buildings, do carpentry work, and purchase provisions for work crews.

Your work will change with the seasons. Planting will be carried out at certain times; harvesting, at others. Most of your work will be outdoors, and you may have to live in the park or forest where you work. You will also have to be ready to handle emergencies in any area of the park, no matter what the weather conditions are. Because you often have to travel long distances in a large park or forest, you should have physical stamina. You will often have to walk on rugged terrain while carrying heavy supplies. Or you may have to ride a horse or travel in a helicopter to cover all the territory in your jurisdiction.

Qualifications

You will need a high school diploma to become a forest technician. Your diploma may be from a vocational high school, but your studies should include math and science. Since you may have to communicate with the public and write reports, you should have solid communication skills, too.

After high school, you should gain at least two years of experience in forestry. This can be accomplished on the job or in school. Valuable work experience includes farming, logging, surveying, or construction. You will also need a driver's license because you will have to drive trucks and maybe even farm equipment, such as tractors.

During your summer vacations, you may want to work in a local park or forest, state conservation bureau, or with the U.S.

Forest Service. The Bureau of Land Management may also have summer jobs available. The National Park Service offers a Volunteers in the Parks (VIP) program for those who wish to try their hand at this work before committing to an actual career. You can apply through any one of the regional offices. Some community and vocational schools now offer two-year courses in general forestry, wildlife, conservation, and forest harvesting. If you combine these courses with field work where you have the opportunity to observe forest work, you will be in a better position to find a job as a forest technician.

Technicians in parks and forests may have a choice of seasonal or temporary work. There will also be more work in the more heavily forested parts of the country. As the economy improves and more people become involved in the recreational and environmental uses of the forest, forest technician jobs may increase.

With your high school diploma and two years of additional schooling, on-the-job experience may put you in line for more responsibilities. But you will need more education if you want to become a forester or park ranger.

It is difficult to predict the career prospects for foresters and technicians because of the economy and demand for paper products. With more individuals and corporations recycling paper products, demand for paper may decrease. Demand for recreational facilities may increase, but you may have to relocate to more heavily forested areas or work for city parks and forests, land developers, or nurseries. You will probably make more money working for private industry than for government, but entry-level salaries will vary with your experience and training.

Federal Government Jobs in Parks

The Department of the Interior administers the National Park Service (NPS), which employs more than twenty thousand permanent and temporary workers and ninety thousand volunteers.

Its mission is to manage and protect more than seventy million acres of natural, cultural, historic, and recreational areas.

Its headquarters is in Washington, D.C., with seven regional offices (Alaska, National Capitol, Southeast, Midwest, Pacific West, Northeast, and Intermountain), an interpretive design center, and a service center. The smallest staff at a park presently is seven, and the largest is more than six hundred. The NPS has 370 sites in the United States, Guam, Puerto Rico, and the Virgin Islands. Temporary jobs are very competitive. Internships are available, and interns are hired by individual parks, so you should determine where you want to work and apply directly. The Student Conservation Association administers three volunteer programs. Resource assistants work for the NPS and other federal agencies. If you choose to work for the NPS, you will have to register with the Office of Personnel Management (OPM). You can contact OPM on-line at www.usajobs.gov. You will have to take a civil service test.

Park Rangers

What Park Rangers Do

At the heart of the park system are the park rangers, whose primary responsibilities include management of wildlife, lakeshores, seashores, and recreation areas. When you first start out, you may be assigned to operate campsites by supplying firewood, assigning sites, and providing security. You may be employed in a city or rural park, and most of your work will be done outdoors.

Much of your work has to do with patrolling the park to prevent unlawful hunting, enforce regulations, inspect trees for disease, and report dangerous situations and emergencies to the park supervisor. Some of your work will also be educating the public on natural and historical features, giving informational speeches, and assisting with research projects.

Park rangers have to instruct the public on safety procedures for water sports, prevention of fires and accidents, and administering first aid. So you'll have to develop good communication skills for educational purposes and also because you may have to settle disputes or clear up misunderstandings among park users.

Qualifications

Park rangers should have at least two years of college with a minimum of twelve credits in science and criminal justice. Courses in natural resource management, natural or earth sciences, park and recreation management, archeology, and anthropology are very helpful. Rangers also receive on-the-job training that is often supplemented with more formal training sessions. Six-month training programs are available at the Grand Canyon National Park in Arizona and at Harpers Ferry, West Virginia. The possibility for promotion would be to district ranger, park manager, or staff specialist. Further education may also be required for these promotions. Jobs with the service are competitive, but the future is looking better because of increased interest in the environment and because of recreational possibilities in the national parks.

Ornithologists

What Ornithologists Do

Ornithologists study birds and may work as teachers, researchers, or outdoor educators. If you decide to become an ornithologist, you will be able to work for federal or state organizations, not-for-profit conservation agencies, in industry, or as a freelancer. You can specialize or be a generalist, work as a wildlife biologist or an endangered species specialist.

All birds are protected by The Migratory Bird Treaty Act, so your work in conservation, preservation of habitat, and protection of species' survival is considered very important for the general health of the environment. It is thought by many that the health of the bird population reflects general environmental health.

Competition for jobs is tight, but there are jobs out there—it just depends on how you want to apply your education and experience. If you want to work outdoors, you'll probably want to work for a governmental agency rather than in a university or museum.

Any experience with birds will be helpful because much of your job as an ornithologist has to do with observing and marking birds. If you are an avid bird watcher, you may have the beginnings of an ornithological career. With that as an avocation, you may want to work as a volunteer or seasonal employee at a park, forest, refuge, zoo, or field station. The more exposure you have to fieldwork or research, the better prepared you will be for your career.

Qualifications

Before you can become an ornithologist, you have to be a biologist with at least a bachelor's degree. In college, you should study anatomy, physiology, ecology, math, and statistics. You may want to pursue study in wildlife biology, zoology, biological sciences, or related fields. If your college offers a course in ornithology, be sure to take it. Your master's degree will mean further course work, writing a thesis and working on a research project that will qualify you to be a professional ornithologist.

Where Ornithologists Work

With governmental agencies, you will be involved in the general field of wildlife management, which includes preservation and study of individual birds and also various species. The U.S. Fish and Wildlife Service administers more than four hundred wildlife refuges, all employing ornithologists. The service also administers research facilities throughout the country. Most national parks also employ ornithologists. You should also check out your state, county, and municipal parks and forest systems.

State conservation agencies need ornithologists, either as part of general wildlife projects or as part of specialized projects concerned with birds only. Field ornithologists are needed for state projects involving endangered and threatened species or status surveys.

Independent organizations focusing on the preservation of bird species are the Nature Conservancy, the National Audubon Society, and the American Bird Conservancy. The Nature Conservancy, founded in 1951, is a leading private international conservation organization. It has more than one million members assisting in the protection of more than eleven million acres in the United States, Canada, Latin America, the Caribbean, Asia, and the Pacific. The Conservancy administers more than thirteen hundred nature sanctuaries and Wings of the Americas, a program that exists to protect critical bird habitats throughout the western hemisphere.

The National Audubon Society and the American Bird Conservancy have partnered to focus on identifying and conserving bird habitats through the Important Bird Areas (IBA) Program. An IBA is defined as a "place that provides essential habitat for one or more species of bird, whether in breeding season, winter, or during migration." More than five hundred such sites have already been identified.

So if birds are your passion, there are opportunities for you if you have the inclination and the education. The professional organization you might want to contact for further information is the American Ornithologists' Union, listed at the end of this chapter.

Range Managers

What Range Managers Do

Managing grazing land for both livestock and wildlife also offers opportunities for employment for nature lovers who want to work outdoors. This land is often called the range, and it also needs managers or conservationists. Often these lands are used for recreation and as natural habitats for animals. As a range manager, you would decide which animals would graze on them and select the proper grazing seasons.

Sometimes you would work as a combination forester, wildlife conservationist, soil erosion specialist, and habitat rehabilitator. You will need to know about vegetation, watershed processes, farming, and ecological interrelationships.

Qualifications

To become a range manager, you need a bachelor's degree in that field. Your course work might include biology, chemistry, physics, plant and animal physiology, and soil sciences. Your knowledge of English and computers as well as wildlife and forestry is helpful.

Where Range Managers Work

Because most of the nation's rangeland is in the West, you may have to relocate to find employment as a range manager. Federal jobs are available through the Forest Service and Bureau of Land Management. State conservation agencies may also provide career opportunities. You can also find employment on privately owned ranches or at universities doing research.

The Society for Range Management

As with any career, it is a good idea to become affiliated with a professional organization. The Society for Range Management was established in 1948 as professional scientific and conservation organization whose mission is "to promote and enhance the stewardship of rangelands to meet human needs based on scientific and sound policy." Land managers, conservationists, scientists, and educators are among its four thousand members. Its publication is called *Rangelands*.

Land Developers Versus Environmentalists

Protecting the wildlife, fish, birds, and trees on the nation's many acres of public and private land requires a wide variety of professionals with a deep commitment to all species affected by change created by humans.

One of the struggles over public lands today is going on between land developers and environmentalists. Developers make their living by building new structures that fill some human need, whether recreational or commercial. Many believe that human needs supersede the needs of all other species. Environmentalists are generally not in complete accord with this belief, and that is where conflicts arise.

The approach to solving such problems is becoming more and more holistic or integrated, with many committed professionals trying to preserve all species in healthy and nurturing habitats. When we lose a species, we know that we will never be able to retrieve it—it is gone forever. It has already happened to many species. Others are hanging on to existence, often in unnatural environments. Many range managers, wildlife managers, biologists, foresters, and park rangers work to reclaim certain habitats or to prevent further destruction through development. Land planners and landscape architects are also called in to investigate the ecology of an area before developers can build a building, a road, a shopping mall, or recreational facility.

New regulations tend to require developers who destroy a wildlife habitat to construct another comparable one. In the case of fish, for example, a new hatchery may need to be constructed. Sometimes a species need not even be threatened or endangered for this to happen.

For this reason, some developers and corporations may hire specialists to restore habitats. These might include wildlife biologists, fish biologists, and culturists. State governments are also becoming aware of habitat problems as new suburban housing developments encroach on homes of deer, beaver, gophers, and raccoons who forage for food in garbage cans because their natural food supply has been destroyed. Or they may move into the garage, basement, or attic, seeking shelter because the trees and bushes that have protected them are gone.

Instead of destroying the wildlife and their habitat, more and more ecologically minded professionals are trying to make sure that new habitats are built or remnants of the old ones are restored. Refuges and sanctuaries also often serve as shelters for displaced animals.

Animal Rehabilitators

What Animal Rehabilitators Do

Sometimes, due to oil spills, land development, highway construction, forest fires, floods, trapping, hunting, or poaching, animals are injured and harmed, shot or maimed. Birds can't fly, fish can't swim. When this happens to wildlife, animal rehabilitators are called in.

Generally speaking, these are usually wildlife and fishery biologists who work at either private or public rehabilitation centers. As a rehabilitator, you would have course work in anatomy and physiology, shock cycles, drugs and medications, and physical therapy. Wounds have to be treated and broken bones mended. Birds, fish, and animals in oil spills have to be thoroughly cleaned before a rehabilitator can care for any other medical problem they may have sustained.

If you can, volunteer at an animal shelter, veterinarian hospital, or state park and work with animals that are under stress, in shock, or injured before you commit yourself to this career. It is difficult to deal with injured animals but necessary in order to preserve and conserve the natural environment. Animal rehabilitators are on the front line of protection and preservation of wildlife, birds, and fish. With the threat of further water, air, and land pollution, the rehabilitator will be in greater demand.

If you are interested in rehabilitating sick and injured animals, you might consider volunteering for an organization like Fellow Mortals. Established in 1985, it is a full-care wildlife rehabilitation center that cares for injured or orphaned animals of all kinds: large and small mammals, birds, and rare animals who are brought there for care until they are released back into the wild. This organization depends on volunteer professionals who take care of animals every day, all year.

Many highly skilled professionals and technicians are needed just to meet today's environmental needs of our forests and parks, wildlife, trees, birds, and fish. Common, as well as endangered, species of animals and plants must be protected as well as livestock, grasslands, and wetlands.

How you want to contribute to the local, state, or federal parks and forests or to private industry or grassroots organizations may depend on how much time you want to devote to education and training and whether you want to specialize in forestry or wildlife biology, ornithology or fish. If you're more comfortable on the ranch or farm, you may want to become a range manager. The future holds many potential changes as land, water, and air continue to be threatened with pollution, development, and technology. Increasing regulations and awareness will necessitate a world full of committed professionals seeking to solve complex environmental problems. You may be one of the lucky ones to participate in the process.

For Further Information

Associations

U.S. Forest Service
U.S. Department of Agriculture
P.O. Box 96090
Washington, DC 20090
www.fs.fed.us/people/employ

National Association of State Foresters
444 North Capitol Street NW, Suite 540
Washington, DC 20001

Society of American Foresters
5400 Grosvenor Lane
Bethesda, MD 20814
www.safnet.org

Soil and Water Conservation Society
7515 Northeast Ankeny Road
Ankeny, IA 50021
www.swcs.org

Student Conservation Association
P.O. Box 550
Charlestown, NH 03603
www.sca-inc.org

Canadian Institute of Forestry
606-151 Slater Street
Ottawa, ON K1P 5H3
Canada
www.cif-ifc.org

The Sierra Club
85 Second Street
San Francisco, CA 94105
www.sierraclub.org

Society for Range Management
445 Union Boulevard, Suite 230
Lakewood, CO 80228
www.srm.org

The Nature Conservancy
4245 North Fairfax Drive
Arlington, VA 22203
www.tnc.org

National Audubon Society
700 Broadway
New York, NY 10003
www.audubon.org

American Bird Conservancy
1250 Twenty-fourth Street NW, Suite 400
Washington, DC 20037
www.abcbirds.org

American Ornithologists' Union
c/o Division of Birds MRC 116
National Museum of Natural History
Washington, DC 20560

Fellow Mortals
W4632 Palmer Road
Lake Geneva, WI 53147
www.fellowmortals.org

CHAPTER SIX

Careers in the Geosciences

E arth scientists are increasingly called geoscientists, and the term includes many different roles. Among their many responsibilities are to study, preserve, and clean the environment. They must observe strict environmental regulations by monitoring waste disposal sites and reclaiming polluted land and water. They try to predict Earth's systems, find natural resources, conserve soils, and determine geological controls on natural resources. They study the earth's past in order to predict its future. Geoscientists are concerned about the land and water on the earth and life on other planets. There is a wide variety of work to do.

According to the National Science Foundation, the major geosciences are geology, geophysics, hydrology, oceanography, marine science, atmospheric science, planetary science, meteorology, environmental science, and soil science. Among these categories, there are also subcategories.

Geologists

If people have told you that you have "rocks in your head," maybe you're cut out to be a geologist! Rocks are exactly what geologists have on their minds, especially in the relationship rocks have to the earth's changes. These natural changes occur through volcanic eruptions, earthquakes, and erosion. So here we are, back to the earth.

What Geologists Do

Geologists study the earth's composition, evolution, past, and future. They do this by investigating rocks and fossils, continental shifts, and natural resources.

Depending on your inclinations, you could become an ecomomic, engineering, glacial, marine, or environmental geologist. Economic geologists study mineral deposits and explore ways to safely dispose of waste as a result of mining. Engineering geologists apply geological data, techniques, and principles to studying soil and groundwater. They want to find out which factors affect buildings, bridges, and dams. Glacial geologists study glaciers and ice sheets, and marine geologists study the ocean floor and basins and coastal environments. Environmental geologists study the geosphere, hydrosphere, atmosphere, and biosphere in order to find out how pollution, waste management, and natural disasters affect human life. Geophysicists apply the principles of physics to study the earth's magnetic, electric, and gravitational fields.

Where Geologists Work

Engineering, gas production, and petroleum companies employ geologists who find most of their work in the United States in the South, the West, and Alaska. You could also work for state, county, or federal governments. The federal agencies that employ geologists are the U.S. Geological Survey (USGS); the U.S. Departments of the Interior, Defense, Agriculture, and Commerce; the Bureaus of Reclamation and Mines; the DeparU.S. tment of Energy; the Forest Service; and the Environmental Protection Agency. With some experience, you may even be able to work as a private consultant.

Qualifications

You will have to be physically strong and like to work under all kinds of climatic conditions if you are going to be a geologist.

When you are in the field, you will have a variety of things to do. Your keen observation skills will be needed for all aspects of your work. You will be using tools, collecting samples, and measuring. You may also be called on to design computer models so that theories can be tested. Geologists in the field usually work together in groups or in teams and have to be able to get along with other people.

If you're still in high school and have those "rocks in your head," you should study English and foreign languages and have a firm footing in math and science. You will eventually have to have a bachelor's degree and maybe even a master's degree. Industrial employers are increasingly looking for the master's degree; university professors and researchers should hold a doctorate.

Suggested courses in college should include chemistry, physics, biology, engineering, and math, in addition to geology. Further study may include hydrology, geophysics, petrology, marine geology, or even paleontology. Many colleges and universities here and in Canada offer degrees in geology, but you should check the requirements and curricula before you select a college or university for undergraduate work.

Salary Outlook

Once you have acquired your education, you will probably find out that the highest salaries are found in the private sector; government generally has a lower pay scale. Salaries vary, of course, but you can probably count on starting at about $34,900 a year with a bachelor's degree and approximately $44,700 with an advanced degree.

Learning about Geology Careers

You may want to work with a state or county agency as a volunteer or part-time worker in order to see if geology is for you.

Since geologists work with other scientists and professionals, you could work in a local park or forest with surveyors or cartographers, urban land planners, or engineers during your summer breaks or vacations. You might also work for a local waste management firm, seismologist, oceanographer, or mineralogist.

This part-time or volunteer work can also give you a better idea about job opportunities in the various areas of specialization in the agency or industry you choose. Many government and industrial organizations have streamlined their operations, and this streamlining may remain in effect in the future. Your education and training will be your best bet in finding a job because the field is becoming more and more technically demanding. Computer and communication skills, laboratory work, and research will also be advantageous in seeking employment.

Professional organizations are also helpful for finding your niche in the work world. Primary among them are the American Geological Institute, the American Association of Petroleum Geologists, and the Geological Society of America. These organizations can provide you with additional information in your search for the rocks and fossils that will make up the rest of your life study as a geologist.

As a nature-loving geologist, much of your effort in the future will be directed toward improvement of our natural resources, including cleaning up any pollution of our water supply. Together with hydrologists and engineers, you will be called upon to contribute to the clean-up process.

Geophysicists

What Geophysicists Do

Also working on environmental problems are geophysicists, who study the earth and apply the principles of physics to its atmosphere, oceans, and space environment. Geophysicists also need knowledge of mathematics and clerical skills. They help us find new sources of energy, understand the climate, study the ocean, and investigate the solar system. Geophysicists look for mineral deposits, study the earth's movements, and probe the evolution of oceans.

Planetologists study the solar system to help us understand the earth; seismologists study earthquakes and explosive shocks under the earth in order to understand their causes; volcanologists study the nature of volcanoes and how they affect the earth's structure. These geophysicists all must have a solid grounding in math and natural science. Physics, chemistry, and geology as well as differential calculus are necessary for any undergraduate course of study.

Qualifications and Education

You should have at least thirty semester hours in mathematics and the physical sciences. Twenty of those hours will include geophysics and physics or math.

Geophysicists should have a good general education because they must be flexible, resourceful, and often willing to travel abroad and work with other professionals. Good communication skills, the ability to work on a team, and facility with the computer are almost essential today for employment. Your work may be in a laboratory or in the field.

Job and Salary Outlook

Through the first years of the twenty-first century, employment for both geologists and geophysicists will probably keep pace with growth in other careers. Since many of these jobs are connected to the petroleum industry, it is subject to changes depending on low oil prices, energy efficiency, and restrictions of drilling.

If geophysics is your choice of career, you may have better opportunities now than in the recent past. The demand for engineering geologists, hydrologists, and geochemists, however, is high.

Working for the U.S. Geological Survey

One of the largest employers in the United States for geoscientists is the U.S. Geological Survey (USGS). Its stated mission is to provide the country with reliable scientific information to:

- describe and understand the earth

- minimize loss of life and property from natural disasters

- manage water, biological, energy, and mineral resources

- enhance and protect our quality of life

The USGS performs its mission by maintaining national and regional databases, analyzing and assessing methods, and conducting research to help sustain adequate natural resources according to environmental standards. Assessment and analysis methods include remote sensing, meteorite research, and mine waste characterization. Mineral process research includes tectonics and metallogenesis of Alaska, geochemical and isotopic studies, and resources and hazards of hydrothermal systems in volcanoes of the Cascade Mountains.

The USGS is presently working on the development of environmental models and tools for economic analysis of mineral deposits, materials flow models, and assessment techniques for industrial materials.

If any of this information interests you, you may want to work for the USGS, which provides various programs that may be what you are looking for. Benefits include:

- flexible work hours

- annual leave accrued up to five weeks of paid time

- family-friendly leave of up to thirteen days of sick leave a year to care for family members

- employee assistance program providing a free counseling and referral service

- travel opportunities

- tuition assistance and tax-deferred retirement benefits

- health benefits, worker's compensation, and life insurance

- competitive salaries

Hydrologists

The environment demands committed work from a variety of professionals, and hydrologists play an integral part in the continuing efforts to maintain the quality of our water. Hydrologists study the location of water on the earth and how it behaves. This study is crucial to our knowledge and understanding of our water supply, how it is used, how much we have, and what forms it takes.

What Hydrologists Do

Hydrologists measure bodies of water and check the amount of underground water, too. Since some of our water comes from snow and rain, hydrologists' work is connected to that of meteorologists. Hydrologists study water as it exists as a liquid, solid, or gas and, therefore, they necessarily work with glaciers, ice, and snow. Since so much water runs through rocks, hydrologists often work with geologists.

Hydrologists collect water samples and analyze them for quantity and quality. They can recommend, based on these results, the most efficient use of the resources we have and predict future needs.

Included in water resource development is water conservation, water quality planning, and the protection of watersheds. Studying water pollution, predicting floods, solving water shortage problems, and forecasting drought are also included. So the hydrologist's work affects everyone's lives and contributes a great deal to the preservation of the environment.

Hydrologists' data also assist in solving water power, irrigation, crop production, and navigation problems. They may also assist in planning farm ponds, sewers, drainage systems, and dams. Erosion, sedimentary deposits, snowfall—all are part of the total picture that the hydrologist must investigate and analyze.

If you become an oceanographic hydrologist, you may assist fishing, shipping, and mining enterprises. You may also be involved in international cooperative ventures since all countries are bound by common oceans, rivers, and lakes and their effects on our lives.

Qualifications

Much of your work will be outdoors with some light to moderate physical work. Good eyesight, creativity, and the ability to share information and work well with others are valuable characteristics for hydrologists. Report writing will also be a part of your job, and, in many cases, knowledge of computers will be necessary.

Hydrologists need to know, among other sciences, chemistry, physics, biology, geology, geophysics, computer science, economics, environmental law, and math. Environmental and mining engineering, ecology, and meteorology are also major components of the mix of disciplines necessary to solve the problems of water resources.

For either the private or public sector, you must have a bachelor's degree with thirty semester hours of course work, including any combination of hydrology, physical sciences, engineering science, soils, math, aquatic biology, and the management or conservation of water resources. Math courses have to include differential and integral calculus and physics. The USGS also recommends studying atmospheric science, meteorology, geology, oceanography, and atmospheric science. It may also accept an appropriate combination of education and experience.

Where Hydrologists Work

Hydrology is said to be one of the hot new career tracks, with many opportunities both in the private and public sectors. A master's degree is in great demand in private industry, which includes consulting and chemical engineering firms and waste disposal firms.

Hydrologists work in forestry, range management, public health, and energy development. They can be found in the mountains or deserts, on farms or in cities. Interrelationships with rocks, dynamics of bodies of water, surface and groundwater, moisture in the soil, sediment, and precipitation all fall in the boundaries of the hydrologists' work.

Government Careers

State and local governments also hire hydrologists, with the primary federal employer being the USGS. The U.S. Forest Service, U.S. Department of Energy, National Oceanic and Atmospheric Administration, the Bureau of Reclamation, and the U.S. Army Corps of Engineers are also employers of hydrologists.

If you work for the USGS, your experience would have to include performing scientific functions on water resources, such as field or laboratory work that requires both application of hydrologic theory and another science. That science might be geology, civil engineering, or geochemistry. These basic requirements would qualify you for the GS-5 level. With more experience and education, you would qualify for the GS-7 level. Both levels would be filled by entry-level hydrologists.

Your salary would depend on your education, experience, and responsibilities. Benefits include:

- paid vacation, sick days, and national holidays
- forty-hour work week with flexible hours
- group medical insurance
- retirement program
- cash awards for outstanding performance
- tuition assistance

State and local governments may provide opportunities for volunteer and part-time work, giving you a chance to explore the possibilities before you commit to the education and training that will be required for full-time employment as a hydrologist. State governments are playing an increasingly more important role in establishing and enforcing regulations to conserve and protect our vital natural resources, including water.

Working alongside hydrologists are hydrologic technicians, who collect, evaluate, compute, and apply their data to various fields. These include engineering, forestry, soil conservation, surveying, and drafting. You may also work in a trade or craft related to hydrological work, such as maintaining equipment.

Working as a Geoscientist for Private Industry

Geoscientists are also employed in private industry. You would probably be working in oil, gas, mining and minerals, or water resources. Some opportunities in private industry are for life scientists, chemists, meteorologists, soil scientists, and mapping

scientists in the business of petroleum and natural gas exploration and extraction. Pay will be higher in the private sector,
but so will the competition. Also, there tends to be less job security in this sector as these industries are vulnerable to recessions
and changes in oil and gas prices, among other factors, and they
usually release workers when exploration and drilling slow down.

Working for State and Local Governments

Part of the reason state governments are employing more people
than in the past is that many of the new environmental laws will
require the expertise of environmental scientists who have thorough knowledge of their own fields and can assist in enforcement
and regulation. States also need people with geologic mapping
skills; an ability to assess resources; and the ability to identify
natural disasters, such as tornadoes, volcanoes, and earthquakes.

Working in Consulting

The consulting industry will be a source of employment for quite
some time for geologists and hydrologists whose work focuses on
the environment. Consulting firms require master's degrees or
bachelor's degrees with appropriate field experience.

Consultants are hired to solve specific problems for their
clients, which means that their communication skills must be
highly developed. Getting your ideas across in "plain English" is
necessary if the nonprofessional client is to understand them.
With that in mind, remember that you may be out in the field
one day and back in the office the next.

Other Employers

Geoscientists in general will also find employment in oil, gas, engineering, and construction companies. Our country needs skilled professional people working to preserve the environment, and these same professionals are needed throughout the world, especially in developing countries that need the technological expertise that these scientists can provide. So it is appropriate that those people who work so closely with the resources of the earth should be able to work anywhere on the earth in order to solve resource problems.

Working in Canada

In 1990, a modification of the Canada/USA Free Trade Act made access to employment for geoscientists in either country possible. You will have to be registered in Canada if you decide to work there. You should contact the Geological Association of Canada before moving. It will provide you with the necessary requirements, regulations, and rules.

Job categories and educational requirements there are similar to those in the United States. Canada is rich in minerals and very concerned about the environment. Canadians are very aware of the need for conservation because of increasing world population, a decreasing supply of natural resources, natural disasters, and man-made catastrophes.

Because of these factors, jobs for geoscientists, both here and in Canada, should be plentiful. If you are well educated in your field; if you have a broad base of academic courses, such as history, languages, and economics; if you are willing to volunteer for fieldwork while you attend school; and if you are versatile enough to combine fields in order to work effectively for the environment, either country should be happy to employ you.

Is a Career in Geosciences for You?

If you're still interested in a career in the earth sciences, you are going to have to commit yourself to your education. You may also want to ask yourself a few questions.

- Do you have an analytical mind?
- Were science courses among your favorites in school?
- Do you like to travel?
- Can you present your ideas coherently?
- Can you see yourself working outdoors in all kinds of weather?
- Do you work well as part of a team?
- Do you like to share your ideas?
- Are you a problem solver?
- Are you curious about the earth and all its changes?
- Are you flexible?

If most answers are "yes," you're ready to look into geoscience careers in government and industry, in the United States, Canada, or throughout the world. The earth is your natural environment, and your job possibilities are excellent.

For Further Information

Associations

American Geophysical Union
2000 Florida Avenue NW
Washington, DC 20009
www.agu.org

Society of Exploration Geophysicists
P.O. Box 70240
Tulsa, OK 74170
www.seg.org

Marine Technology Society
1828 L Street, Suite 906
Washington, DC 20036
www.mtsociety.org

American Geological Institute
4220 King Street
Alexandria, VA 22302
www.agiweb.org

American Association of Petroleum Geologists
P.O. Box 979
Tulsa, OK 74101
www.aapg.org

Geological Society of America
3300 Penrose Place
P.O. Box 9140
Boulder, CO 80301
www.geosociety.org

Publications

For copies of the free publications listed below, contact the USGS Information Services office:

USGS Information Services
Box 25286
Denver, CO 80225

Collecting Rocks

Natural Gemstones

Acid Rain and Our Nation's Capital—A Guide to Effects on Buildings and Monuments

Groundwater and the Rural Homeowner

The Geology of Radon

Water Use in the United States

Coasts in Crisis

Are Fertilizers and Pesticides in the Groundwater? A Case Study of the Delmarva Peninsula, Delaware, Maryland, and Virginia

Our Changing Landscape—Indiana Dunes National Lakeshore

Understanding Our Fragile Environment—Lessons from Geochemical Studies

The Future of Energy Gases

Tapping the Earth's Natural Heat

Look Before You Build

For a copy of the publication *Gemstones* and selected references on rocks, minerals, and gemstones, write to:

Superintendent of Documents
P.O. Box 371954
Pittsburgh, PA 15250

CHAPTER SEVEN

The Need for Pollution Control and Waste Management

F rom all the careers that we have looked at so far, it becomes increasingly clear that preserving the environment demands sophisticated methods and combined efforts. Professionals must work as teams to reverse threats to the earth's resources. Two of the most crucial tasks for those of you who want to make a career of preserving the earth are pollution control and waste management.

No one is isolated from environmental problems. They affect us all. Public/private partnerships are formed so that we can ensure a clean environment for future generations. States work with the federal government, industry is contracted by the federal government, and environmental organizations work with international agencies to resolve common problems. Watchdog groups look for inadequacies in governmental regulations and try to correct them. Because pollution is a global problem, national governments have devised regulations and enforcements that seek to curb any further damage to the land, air, and water we depend on for life and sustenance.

The Environmental Protection Agency

In the United States, the agency to set regulations and enforce punishment for polluters is the Environmental Protection

Agency (EPA). It was formed in 1970 because the American public became increasingly aware of the danger of pollution. It was formed by transferring staff from the Departments of the Interior; Health, Education, and Welfare; Agriculture; Food and Drug Administration; and the Atomic Energy Commission. At that time, a little more than five thousand people worked for the EPA; today, more than seventeen thousand are employed by the EPA. Today, the EPA administers ten regions covering all fifty states. Though the mission of the EPA—"to protect human health and the environment"—remains the same, new challenges have arisen in the years since its inception. It is worthwhile to look into the EPA for career opportunities for permanent full-time jobs as well as internships, fellowships, and student programs.

The National Network for Environmental Management Studies (NNEMS), a program of the EPA, offers students fellowships for practical research experiences that allow them to work during the summer or during the school year. These fellowships are offered in Environmental Policy, Regulation, and Law; Environmental Management and Administration; Environmental Science; Public Relations and Communications; and Computer Programming and Development. Fellowships are awarded to undergraduate and graduate students who meet eligibility criteria. You can find application forms at the career service center of participating universities and check the website for further information: www.epa.gov/enviroed/NNEMS.

In conjunction with the Environmental Careers Organization, the EPA sponsors the Student Environmental Associate Program and Diversity Initiative, bringing in talented young people from many different communities and tribes throughout the United States. The paid training sessions last from three to six months, and participants are chosen based on their academic records, extracurricular activities, and intention to pursue an environmental career. For an application form, contact:

The Environmental Careers Organization
179 South Street
Boston, MA 02111

The EPA's Tribal Lands Environmental Science Scholarship Program enables Native Americans to compete for scholarships in environmental science. The students are judged on certain criteria, including grade point, knowledge of their culture, intent to work for the environment, and leadership. If you want further information, contact:

The American Indian Science and Engineering Society (AISES)
1630 Thirtieth Street, Suite 301
Boulder, CO 80301

Another EPA program targeting talented young people is its National Center for Environmental Research and Quality Assurance. This program seeks to motivate students to commit to careers in the environment and to enhance the work of practicing environmentalists with visiting scientist programs.

Because of the nature and scope of the mission of the EPA and the many environmental problems that we face, it is a place you may start in determining your career track. Because the problems are challenging, it will take highly sophisticated skills and knowledge to know how to cope with the enormity and global aspect of environmental science. The better educated you are, the better the chance you will have to find a good and lasting career in the environmental sciences.

The Problem of Water Pollution

Water pollution is one of the most serious problems that we face because water recycles itself. We have virtually the same amount of water today that we will have in the future. Therefore, we have to be sure that the water we drink or in which organisms must survive remains pure and clean. This is a difficult task because so much of our water is already polluted, and the danger of accidental pollution from oil and other spills is always present.

Several laws do help us control damage to our waterways: the River and Harbor Act of 1899, the Water Quality Act of 1965, the Clean Water Restoration Act of 1966, the Federal Water Pollution Control Act Amendments of 1972, the Clean Water Act of 1977, the Safe Drinking Water Act of 1974 (amended in 1977 and 1986), and the Water Quality Act of 1987. All of this legislation provides standards of purity for interstate, coastal, and drinking water. These laws were passed to assure that no industry could discharge pollutant material into water without permission and that waste material would be pretreated so as not to harm city treatment facilities. They also assure the quality of the taste and odor of drinking water and mandate that drinking water be clean enough to prevent disease.

Wastewater has to be treated for reuse in a treatment plant, usually through sewers or septic tanks. Solids are removed, and then the water is purified through certain biological processes. If the water is still not clean enough, further purification is necessary. In the process, sludge is produced, which is often used as fertilizer. Other uses of sludge are being studied.

Careers in Water Pollution Control

Because of the expanding global population and resulting industrial waste, jobs in water pollution control should be quite plentiful in the coming years. Again, a wide range of career opportunities await you, depending on the time you are willing to devote to education and training and whether you want to work for government, industry, or independent organizations.

Land planners, citizens, chemists, engineers, technicians, government agencies, private industries, and biologists—all are needed to help reduce waste, to clean up existing waste, and to look for solutions for the future.

Let's start with the possibilities with the federal government and, more particularly, with the Environmental Protection Agency to see which jobs are listed for your consideration. We will divide career paths into two categories: water treatment and wastewater treatment careers. Water-treatment jobs deal with unused or raw water; wastewater is used water that can be returned to rivers or lakes once treated.

Water-Treatment Jobs

Pump-Station Operators

Treatment plants need pump-station operators, whose work will often take them outdoors. Water from rivers, lakes, or other sources has to be pumped to the plant and then to the users of the purified water. Often millions of gallons of water are pumped daily through a series of storage tanks, conduits, and mains. The pumps are operated and controlled by pump-station operators.

All the equipment must be in good working order to allow for the proper amount of pressure, flow, and level of water for the needs of consumers. Pump-station operators have to know how to conduct tests and keep records of this information. They also have to be able to work with their hands and be familiar with tools.

If you think you would like to be a pump-station operator, you will probably be required to have a high school diploma, preferably with some experience operating and maintaining equipment. You may also want to investigate two-year colleges that offer an associate degree in environmental technology.

You would probably start out as a helper or maintenance worker, during which time you would be trained. After about six months, you might advance to water-treatment plant operator. Most of these jobs are available at city treatment plants.

Water-Treatment Plant Operators

Water-treatment plant operators are similar to pump-station operators, except that they maintain the purity of the water by monitoring panels to check pressure, level, and flow of the water as it moves through the pumps. They must add substances to the water and then test it for purity, clarity, and odor. This operator has to keep accurate records and maintain equipment.

These jobs are usually available at treatment plants in large cities and individual communities. Your job duties may vary according to the size of the facility, and the staff size will also vary. If you work in a very small town, your work may be only part time. Considering, however, all the regulations concerning water quality, these jobs will be plentiful for quite some time.

To become a water-treatment plant operator, you will probably have to have a high school diploma or a comparable mix of education and experience. It is an advantage if you have had some jobs handling machinery and mechanical equipment.

Vocational schools may offer courses in water treatment, and you can also check community colleges for environmental technology courses. The more education, training, and experience you have, the better your career opportunities will be. You may also be required to take a civil service exam after you have completed your training. Most operators also have to be certified.

As an apprentice, you will need on-the-job training. In some cases, you may also have to update your knowledge through seminars in order to renew your license. Some states offer courses or specialized training to help you with new technology. These may include aquatic biology, new regulations, or record keeping.

Check with your state licensing board for certification laws and required training.

Your job prospects look good and should remain steady in the coming years, especially if you continue to update your skills and knowledge. From operator, you could be promoted to foreman, supervisor, or superintendent.

Water Filter Cleaners

Another technical job in the water treatment plant is the water filter cleaner. The water filter cleaner is responsible for keeping the water at the bottom of the filter basin clean. These basins hold layers of gravel and sand through which the water is filtered so that it comes out pure in the end.

The sand and gravel are removed with a suction pipe operated by the filter cleaner, who then hoses the sand and gravel to remove any impurities, scrapes the filter bed, and returns the clean sand and gravel to the bed. You might guess that the filter cleaner has to be physically strong—and you would be right. Filter cleaners often have to work outside the plant in sometimes less-than-comfortable surroundings.

Although this job is essential in the water purification process, it doesn't require a great deal of education, and you would receive on-the-job training. You should be reliable and industrious to tackle this kind of work. Your best employment opportunity will probably be with large filtration plants. This is a good ground-level job to see if you would like to become a mechanic's helper or water-treatment plant operator.

Wastewater Treatment Jobs

Many of the same processes take place for the treatment of wastewater, but in this case, sewers bring used water to the plant for cleaning and reuse. Many of these plants employ chemists, microbiologists, and a variety of other workers in addition to plant operators. Since chemists and microbiologists work mainly in laboratories, we'll concentrate on those job opportunities that are found, for the most part, outside the office or laboratory.

Industrial Waste Inspectors

For example, the industrial waste inspector goes to the origin of the pollutants—the industrial or commercial site where the pollutants are treated for disposal—to make sure that permits are valid, and that equipment is up to standard, and sometimes to collect samples of the water for testing. Any water source, such as a river, lake, or stream, has to be tested to be sure that harmful pollutants are not discharged into them from a commercial site.

Samples are also collected from sewers and drains and tested in the laboratory. Certain field tests are taken on the spot, such as those for acidity and alkalinity. Most inspectors are also required to take complaints, help industry owners with compliance to regulations, and keep accurate and thorough records in order to calculate any surcharges an offending company may have to pay.

As an inspector, you will be required to do quite a bit of fieldwork and will be exposed to various weather conditions. You will also have to do some light physical work—climbing, walking, crawling, or stretching. Because you are looking for violations of environmental regulations, you must be able to instruct people who are responsible for following the rules while strictly enforcing them. You may be called on to work closely with officers of a company to educate them in federal and state regulations—which can sometimes be confusing—and help them come up with solutions.

To become an industrial waste inspector, you will need to have a good background in wastewater plant operations, know the current environmental regulations, and have a knowledge of equipment and machinery. Very often this position is a promotion from wastewater treatment plant operator. And with further education and training, you could become a supervisor or manager. Since water quality control is becoming increasingly important in this country, you should have a steady job, especially in big cities or near large industrial sites.

Industrial Waste Samplers

Industrial waste samplers are workers who go directly to the water source and take used and unused samples to the plant for chemical analysis. These samples are usually taken from suspicious locations, put into tubes or bottles, and labeled with the pertinent information. If the samples indicate that a certain industry has not followed regulations, these samples will help to determine the amount of fines that will be charged to the offending industry.

Sometimes tests are made on site, or monitoring devices are set up to record conditions at specific times and to measure water flow and pressure. Samplers have to be prepared to climb, bend, stretch, and stoop in order to get the samples, so they should be in good physical shape. Both inspectors and samplers need to know how to drive a car and in some cases to operate a small boat.

Some technical training at a vocational high school or courses in wastewater treatment can get you in the door. Then you will have on-the-job training with more experienced personnel. If you want to go further in your career, you will have to get more formal education in wastewater treatment. The outlook for the future is good because of the need to enforce pollution laws and the increasing responsibility of the states in enforcement procedures.

Sewage Disposal Workers

The sewage disposal worker makes sure that all filters, pumps, screens, and tanks are clean by hosing, brushing, and using cleaning solutions. This work is done outdoors for the most part and requires physical stamina, at least an eighth-grade education, and a high degree of reliability and dependability. On-the-job training can be accomplished in about a month.

Sewer Maintenance Workers

Sewers, including manholes, storm drains, and pipes, have to be maintained and repaired on a regular basis, and this is the job of the sewer maintenance worker. They perform routine maintenance as well as replace sections that have worn out. They use power tools, power rodders, high-velocity water jets, and flushers.

This job requires hard, physical labor, such as cutting trees, removing debris, and climbing into manholes. These workers have to bend, stoop, climb, kneel, and crawl in all kinds of weather in the midst of many different, often unpleasant, odors.

A high school diploma is preferred for this work, and you should count on a six-month, on-the-job training period. You could be promoted, after you have accumulated some experience, to lead worker and then to maintenance equipment operator.

Mechanics

Mechanics in the wastewater treatment plant are responsible for the maintenance and repair of all machines and equipment, including electric motors, turbines, pumps, and blowers. Sometimes they may have to operate the equipment. If you decide to become a mechanic, you'll have to be familiar with power tools, wrenches, and hoists and carry many of them with you as you perform your tasks. This will require some physical strength because you will be crawling, kneeling, and climbing, both inside and outside.

You'll also have to have an aptitude for mechanical work and a high school diploma for this job. Vocational or trade school background is helpful, and there are apprenticeship programs available. With further education, experience, and certification, you could become a superintendent of a wastewater treatment plant.

Plant Attendants

Plant attendants have to adjust pipe valves, watch temperature and flow rates, turn on steam valves, and inform the superintendent of any trouble. Sometimes they are called on to collect samples and repair equipment. They may also have to perform general maintenance work as well as record keeping. Two years of high school are sufficient for the job, with three to six months' training for an entry-level position. With further education and experience, you may qualify for certification for wastewater treatment plant operator.

Wastewater Treatment Plant Operators

This job is similar to that of the water treatment plant operator. These workers control and operate the pumps, pipes, and valves. The flow of water and solid wastes must be monitored in order for the proper amount of chemicals and wastewater to be processed. Pumps and generators have to be stopped and started, and heat and electricity must be provided to the plant itself. In addition, all equipment has to be inspected for possible repairs. This is the work of the operator.

In large plants, the operators may specialize, for example, as sludge-control operators or sludge-filtration operators. In other plants, operators may be called on to perform general maintenance of buildings, prepare laboratory tests, and be on call for emergencies.

As a plant operator, you may be working in all kinds of weather, and you may be crawling, climbing, kneeling, and crouching on the job. You will also have to know how to use common and specialized tools and be able to read blueprints.

You'll need a high school diploma and two years of experience in equipment maintenance. If you enter an apprenticeship program, you'll get courses in mathematics, physics, and chemistry. You may also need three years of experience in addition to this classroom training. If you attend a two-year college, you should get an associate's degree in environmental technology. Courses include math, social science, computer science, communications, report writing, and wastewater treatment. You will have to pass a written test for certification in most states.

Job possibilities as a wastewater treatment plant operator look bright for the future, especially in large cities and as state employees, mainly because of the increasing awareness and new regulations both on the local and state levels.

Supervisors

Supervisors of water and sewer systems are in charge of planning and coordinating all activities in the sewage system, including excavating culverts, installing sewer mains, drilling taps, and making street repairs. As a supervisor, you'll have to keep accurate records, read land plots, order materials, and maintain and repair all equipment. Much of your work will have to do with executing projects and supervising the work of others.

Most of your work will be done outdoors and will demand good physical strength, eyesight, and hearing. A high school diploma is preferred, but you can rise through the ranks to become a supervisor. An aptitude for mechanics, mathematics, or shop in a trade or vocational school is very helpful.

Estuarial Technicians

Other technicians are needed in water quality control, such as the estuarine resource technician and the water pollution control technician. Estuaries, such as bays, inlets, and lagoons, need to be studied for quality because of the rich variety of wildlife that they maintain. As an estuarial technician, you may have to wear diving gear to collect water samples for laboratory analysis. You will also be responsible for writing reports, working with other professionals, and operating instruments that are used in collecting samples.

A two-year associate's degree with course work in math, biology, marine instrumentation, computer science, chemistry, and English is helpful. You should also have laboratory work, ecology, and statistical analysis courses. You will probably have to have a bachelor's degree to be promoted.

Water Pollution Control Technicians

Water pollution control technicians take samples from a variety of water sources, monitor flow and other information, operate measuring devices, and conduct on-site chemical and physical tests to help control pollutants in raw or used water. They then have to write up thorough reports of this fieldwork. They often have to interpret computer printouts, prepare statistical analyses of the results, and prepare materials to be used by engineers, scientists, or environmentalists. Most of their work is done outdoors, sometimes under difficult conditions. Therefore, good physical condition is important as well as the willingness to travel a great deal.

An associate's degree in chemical technology or science is recommended for this job. It is also important to have at least one year of experience with surveying, measuring, or testing equipment. College courses should include math, natural sciences, chemistry, biology, and engineering. You will receive training with an engineer or scientist and could achieve advancement with a bachelor's degree in engineering or science.

Environmental Engineers

Engineering professionals are in great demand for water-quality control careers. Both government and industry are looking for environmental engineers. As an environmental engineer, you could enter the field of water pollution control, air pollution control, or solid waste management. Your job, in any case, is to lend engineering principles and practice to environmental control systems through analysis and synthesis.

You will determine the effects of humans on natural and man-made environments, studying the cause and effect of all forms of pollution and the management of solid wastes. You will try to minimize toxic levels of waste materials through research and development of new technologies. You may work with social and applied scientists and members of the public.

You may design processes for waste treatment to acceptable standards and figure out ways to make work environments safer. In the process, you may have to write reports and make presentations. Therefore, your communications skills have to be strong, as well as your computer and design skills. You will also have to be able to work with a wide range of people in different areas to mutually solve problems.

As an undergraduate, you might study thermodynamics, water resources and geotechnical engineering, fluid mechanics, and heat transfer. You would also probably have opportunities to solve real-life problems in laboratories to prepare you for problems you would find on the job. If you choose water pollution control or solid waste management, your studies will include waste characteristics and the engineering of treatment processes and equipment.

Sanitary Engineers

Sanitary engineers are responsible for sewage disposal, water pollution control, or water supply problems. They also assist in watershed development and aqueduct and filtration plant construction. Sewage problems involving waste treatment plants are investigated, samples are taken, and evaluations made. These engineers may also be in charge of water supply programs for government agencies. They sometimes work at construction sites, where they advise industrial and civic leaders about wastewater treatment regulations and develop waste treatment programs.

In college, you should graduate as a civil engineer and then take a master's degree in sanitary engineering. Or you may have chemical, structural, or public health engineering as an undergraduate major. Most states require that you be registered and licensed before you start your career. As a sanitary engineer, your services will be needed in private industry as a consultant to architectural firms or for major municipal wastewater treatment plants, environmental organizations, and health departments.

Hydrologic Engineers

Hydrologic engineers deal with construction of dams, aqueducts, and reservoirs for the use and control of water supplies. They study soil drainage, flooding, and conservation and analyze droughts, storms, and flood runoff records to forecast and prevent floods and plan for water storage during periods of drought. Some specialize in irrigation projects for agricultural purposes. Hydrologic engineers need a bachelor's degree in civil engineering and should have two years of experience in related work.

Oil Pollution Control Engineers

Oil pollution control engineers are responsible for prevention and control of oil spills. In worst-case scenarios, when the spill actually occurs, they plan for the cleanup and disposal of the spill. Complete prevention of oil spills may be impossible, but engineers can determine monitoring and maintenance programs for equipment and machinery and develop inspection programs for personnel to check for leaks and malfunctions. Engineers inform appropriate personnel about tides, currents, and wind patterns; they monitor those sites where oil spills might occur; and they help gas station attendants know how to control and monitor spills in tanks, drains, and catch basins.

Plans for containment and cleanup of oil spills, once they occur, have to be made individually, sometimes depending on whether they are on or offshore. But the engineers' decisions have to be made immediately, according to how fast the oil is dispersed, what the velocity of the wind is, and how fast the water current is. The shape of the spill and length of time that it will take to get all the contractors and helpers to the site have to be considered. Often training drills with a crew will have to take place beforehand to estimate response time in case of emergency.

In the cleanup process, the engineer has many things to think about: keeping accurate records, collecting samples, informing wildlife agencies if necessary, maintaining all environmental rules and regulations, coordinating with local fire departments, and alerting local authorities to the potential hazards to water sources in the affected areas. After the cleanup, the engineer arranges for disposal of the recovered oil. Some of your work would be indoors, but in emergencies, you would be called on to work at the site of the spill, sometimes in bad weather and unpleasant conditions.

A combination of a bachelor's degree in petroleum, chemical, or civil engineering and a long career in all phases of pollution control are necessary for the job of oil pollution control engineer. Then you will be qualified to work for oil companies; contractors who specialize in cleanup; and any federal or state governmental agency that is responsible for the prevention, control, cleanup, and disposal of oil spills.

Civil Engineers

Civil engineers who study the physical control of water work to prevent floods, direct river flow, and control water supply for irrigation purposes. If canals, locks, or hydroelectric power systems are needed, they construct them.

Other careers associated with supplying water for irrigation are basin operators, ditch riders, and watershed tenders. Basin operators remove silt and sand from river water before the water can be used. They may operate certain equipment and keep records. Ditch riders help determine how much water is needed and how long it will be needed. They often have to patrol areas to look for leaks or impediments, clear brush, or repair gauges and meters. Watershed tenders control water flow from reservoirs through the use of gauges and meters. They also keep records, maintain equipment, and solve problems.

All these careers—from providing quality water to controlling its flow to cleaning it up after disasters—show a concern for the tenuous nature of one of our most valuable natural resources. Large numbers of professionals and technicians are needed now and in the future to maintain water purity for agricultural, residential, commercial, and industrial use.

If you choose to be a civil engineer, you will need a bachelor's degree with course work in surveying, structural engineering, hydraulics, and transportation planning in addition to basic sciences, math, and the humanities. Many programs emphasize a team design approach to solving problems.

The Problem of Land Pollution

Land is abused in many ways on a daily basis throughout the world. One of the most pressing problems at the moment is garbage disposal. We are presently producing more solid waste than we can dispose of. The words *dumping* and *landfill* are familiar to all of us. Ordinary garbage pollutes the land and groundwater, and the contaminants are carried through the air by insects outside the dump itself. Dumps become health hazards to humans, housing disease-carrying rodents and vermin.

More dangerous to the land are the hazardous waste sites, which can be found throughout the country. A monumental job lies ahead for environmental professionals in disposing of such waste, containing it, or converting it to nonhazardous sub-stances. These solid waste problems are so dangerous to the sur-vival of our planet that it will take a concerted effort on the part of every consumer, industry, grassroots organization, environ-mental professional, and government agency to turn things around for this good Earth.

The laws on the books now are helpful, but the problem deserves the total commitment of all citizens to accomplish the kinds of results we need. In 1965, the Solid Waste Disposal Act opened the door for the development of programs that tackled the problem of disposal and provided states with financial and technical aid to carry them out.

The Resource Conservation and Recovery Act of 1970 pro-vided financial aid to construct disposal facilities and research possibilities for the management of solid waste. The Research Conservation and Recovery Act of 1976 further expanded on recovering energy from disposed materials and establishing regu-lations for the management of hazardous wastes. The Superfund was established specifically to clean up hazardous waste sites that are already in existence. An understanding of these and other federal and local laws is crucial to anyone interested in working for the preservation and purification of Mother Earth.

Individual states are becoming more and more responsible for environmental protection of their area. Part of this mission is to recover resources and energy that had been discarded. Local gov-ernments, grassroots organizations, and individual companies are setting up recycling centers in most cities. And garbage collect-ing in many areas has been separated for more rapid recycling. Sanitary landfills have become the norm so that solid waste is disposed of within layers and then covered over to reduce pollu-tants. Consumers are demanding of manufacturers that they reduce their packaging, and whole industries have at least become aware of the "green revolution." Citizens are now very aware of how dangerous nuclear waste sites are to their health and well-being.

Careers in Land Pollution

Waste Management Engineers

Careers with solid waste management and hazardous waste cleanup are many. At the forefront are waste management engineers, who study specifications and plans, inspect disposal facilities, recommend the best ways to process and dispose of garbage, and develop recovery resources programs. They write reports and advise appropriate people in government or industry on rules and regulations regarding waste disposal.

A combination of a bachelor's degree and waste management work experience or a master's degree in waste management engineering will qualify you for a position in this field. With growing interest in this area, your prospects for a solid career are very good.

Waste Management Specialists

Alongside the engineers are the waste management specialists. Although they don't design programs, they inspect landfills, confer with appropriate health officials, advise those who operate sanitary landfills on improved methods of disposal, take complaints, and prepare reports. You can qualify for this position with a bachelor's degree in environmental science or civil, sanitary, or chemical engineering. Some experience in solid waste management is preferred.

The Problem of Air Pollution

The air that we and other species depend on for life is also being polluted—with recent EPA estimates of millions of tons of fumes and soot produced each year in the United States alone. Cars, houses, and smokestacks add carbon monoxide, sulfur dioxide, lead, asbestos, and even arsenic to the air we breathe. Our lungs are at risk on a daily basis when we inhale the smoke from cigarettes or are exposed to radon or asbestos in the buildings we live or work in.

Nuclear accidents like those at Three Mile Island and Chernobyl further add to the problem. Prevention and control of air pollution is a top priority here and in every country in the world.

The Clean Air Act of 1970, with amendments in 1974 and 1977, was designed to force states to develop programs to control air pollution and conform to federal clean air standards. Even now we do not have the ozone and carbon monoxide problems solved, even though most other pollutants, such as nitrogen dioxide and sulfur dioxide, are now within federal standards.

Ozone depletion is associated with the greenhouse effect, which is seen by many to be a top priority for all air pollution professionals. Toxic wastes, such as dioxin and PCBs, also contribute to hazardous health conditions. All this is combined with the problems of pesticides, radon, and other carcinogenic compounds found in inside air to form a monumental global crisis.

Careers in Air Pollution

Air Quality Engineers

If you are feeling committed enough to explore the career possibilities in air quality and pollution control, you should know that the need for environmental professionals is great and will be so in the future. For example, air quality engineers are needed in governmental agencies, private industry, oil refineries, electric power plants, and in consulting firms. Their responsibilities include visiting industrial sites, investigating trouble areas, making recommendations for improvements, and setting deadlines for compliance. They also plan new construction, with reduction of pollution as a primary objective. These plans may be for a commercial plant, power plant, or highway. They consider traffic patterns, climate, housing, and even wind direction when making recommendations for new construction.

Some air quality engineers design testing devices, devise new pollution-reducing processes, or explore ways to remove pollutants from certain substances. They work indoors and outdoors, are on call in emergencies, and have the ability to solve problems and do research. Many have to travel to specific sites on a regular basis and often have to climb, lift, and otherwise perform in various climatic conditions.

To qualify as an air quality engineer, you'll have to have a bachelor's degree in engineering and be certified as a professional engineer. If you work for the government, you will have to pass the civil service exam.

Chemical Engineers

Chemical engineers, like environmental and civil engineers, are in demand in both government and industry, helping to solve air pollution control problems. They work in the manufacturing, pharmaceutical, biotechnology, and environmental safety industries. Among government agencies that hire chemical engineers are the EPA and the Departments of the Interior, Commerce, and Agriculture; the U.S. Army; and the Nuclear Regulatory Commission. Chemical engineers need a college or university degree, with grounding in sciences, math, and computers.

Air Quality Specialists

Air quality specialists go into the field to inspect, test, and analyze pollution sources, take samples of soil and other materials affected by air pollution, and write up reports and recommendations. They assist in environmental impact statements, take complaints on hazards caused by toxic waste, and assist in enforc-ing environmental protection regulations.

A bachelor's degree in science, engineering, environmental health, or statistics is necessary to qualify as an air quality spe-cialist. You should study chemistry, physics, and biology as an undergraduate. Knowledge of computers, public administration, and environmental studies is also beneficial. You will probably also receive on-the-job training whether you work for the gov-ernment, industry, or consulting firms.

Air Quality Technicians

Air quality technicians assist engineers and scientists by collect-ing air samples, testing them for pollutants, and recording the information. They inspect pollution sources, test air quality, and operate electronic equipment. Much of this work is done on site and often involves repairing equipment, drawing graphs, and making mathematical equations.

You may prefer to specialize in meteorological work as an air quality technician. As such, you would work with meteorologists in forecasting levels of air pollution. You would work at test sites to check equipment and record temperatures, wind velocity and direction, and pressure. You would assist the meteorologist in set-ting up weather instruments, performing mathematical calcula-tions, and working with maps and graphs.

You will need two years of college or technical training. This should include laboratory, mechanical, and electrical experience. You will also have to know air quality regulations.

The time is now for you to get involved in pollution control and waste management. No three areas could be more important than the water, the land, and the air for the preservation and conservation of our environment. No cause could be more important than cleaning up and purifying those elements that allow us to live.

For Further Information

Associations

American Institute of Chemical Engineers
3 Park Avenue
New York, NY 10016
www.aiche.org

Association for Experiential Education
Jobs Clearing House
2305 Canyon Boulevard, Suite 100
Boulder, CO 80302
www.aee.org

Environmental Careers Organization
179 South Street
Boston, MA 02111
www.eco.org
   Publication: *Connections* newsletter

National Wildlife Federation
1400 Sixteenth Street NW
Washington, DC 20036
www.nwf.org
   Publication: *Conservation Directory*

Student Conservation Association
P.O. Box 550
Charlestown, NH 03603
www.sca-inc.org
   Publication: *Earth Works Magazine*

Publications

Basta, Nicholas. *The Environmental Career Guide*. John Wiley Press, 1992.

Cohn, Susan, and Horst Rechelbacher. *Green at Work: Finding a Business Career That Works for the Environment*. Island Press, 1992.

Earth Work: Resource Guide to Nationwide Green Jobs. Harper Collins West, 1994.

Doyle, Kevin. *The Complete Guide to Environmental Careers in the 21st Century*. Environmental Careers Organization, 1999.

Job Opportunities: The Environment. Peterson's Guides, 1994.

About the Author

Along with the rest of you, Louise Miller is concerned with the preservation of the planet and the conservation of natural resources. Besides recycling, shopping carefully, and not eating meat, Miller is also trying to spread the word about reducing, reusing, and recycling.

In addition to nature, Miller also loves languages, especially English and German. She started out as a German teacher and teaches it today, after having studied in Vienna, Austria, and Bonn, Germany. She has also taught German at the Universities of Kansas, Missouri, and Illinois.

Her love of English led her to teaching, writing, editing, and proofreading the language. She has taught English at community and business colleges, conducts writing and ESL workshops, and has worked both full-time and freelance for publishing houses. These include Compton's Encyclopedia, Rand McNally & Company, American Library Association, and World Book. Miller was also research coordinator for television quiz shows in Los Angeles and has written a wildlife column for the Woodstock (Illinois) *Sentinel*.

Miller is currently communications coordinator for a large social service agency.